FAITH
ON TRIAL

Pamela Binnings Ewen

FAITH
ON TRIAL

PAMELA BINNINGS EWEN

BROADMAN
& HOLMAN
PUBLISHERS

Nashville, Tennessee

0–8054–2026–6 (pbk.)

Published by Broadman & Holman Publishers, Nashville, Tennessee
Editorial Team: Leonard G. Goss, John Landers, Sandra Bryer
Page Design and Typesetting: PerfecType, Nashville, Tennessee

Dewey Decimal Classification: 232
Subject Heading: LAW/RELIGION/HISTORY

Unless otherwise noted, Scripture quotations are from the
NEW AMERICAN STANDARD BIBLE,
© Copyright The Lockman Foundation, 1960, 1962, 1963,
1968, 1971, 1972, 1973, 1975, 1977, 1995.
Citations marked NIV are from the Holy Bible, New International Version,
© copyright 1973, 1978, 1984.
Citations marked RSV are from the *Revised Standard Version of the Bible,*
copyrighted 1946, 1952, © 1971, 1973.

Library of Congress Cataloging-in-Publication Data

Ewen, Pamela Binnings, 1944–
    Faith on trial : an attorney analyzes the evidence for the life,
death & Resurrection of Jesus of Nazareth / by Pamela Binnings Ewen.
    p. cm.
    Includes bibliographical references.
    ISBN 0-8054-2026-6 (pbk.)
    1. Jesus Christ—Resurrection. 2. Bible. N.T. Gospels—Evidences,
authority, etc. I. Title.
BT481.E94   1999
232.9'08—dc21

                                                        99–19136
                                                        CIP

2 3 4 5 03 02 01 00 99

To

John and Scott

Contents

Preface

This book was written for those on the outside looking in—those who seek the comfort that religion has to offer but need a rational foundation for belief. It is the result of a fifteen year search for truth, which I began as an agnostic.

Imagine yourself looking through a window at a garden. It is full of flowers but it appears murky, dark and gray to you. Someone remarks that it is really very colorful, shimmering with sunlight and exceptionally beautiful. Now this may seem to you a pure absurdity because your ordinary consciousness tells you otherwise. Even the *will* to believe cannot overcome your perception of reality. But if you are shown that your vision has been obscured because the window is made of the darkest filtered glass, then by opening the window you will see clearly the radiance of the colorful garden.

The heart will not accept what the mind rejects. But by *reason* doubt can be cleared away and truth can be illuminated. This is what the book attempts to do, through the presentation of evidence examined under standards that are applicable in a court of law in the United States of America.

Acknowledgments

I would like to thank my cousin Elizabeth Nell Dubus for taking the time to read the manuscript of this book and for her thoughtful suggestions; Mary Dix for all of her assistance in polishing and refining; my editor Len Goss, who asked for answers to the toughest questions; my friend and agent, Kathleen Davis Niendorff, who added depth and grace to the words on the pages; my husband, John, for his patience and understanding; and my mother Barbara Perkins Binnings, for always providing a gentle guiding light.

Introduction

Faith is a wonderful gift, but it was not given to me. At the point that one begins to wonder what life is really all about and when the music will stop, this becomes an unacceptable state of affairs. Without faith in a loving God and eternal life, we must eventually face our most primal fear—that this is all there is. Are we merely here for a meaningless moment? Perhaps it really is true that our days on earth are like grass, that like wildflowers we bloom and die—the wind blows and we are gone, as though we had never been.

But all that I have implied is a *desire* to believe in God and life after death. You cannot will yourself into a position of faith, but you can open your mind and search for the truth. A search like that will lead you into fascinating avenues of information—science, the arts, archaeology, medicine. All contribute small pieces of the puzzle which together present an intriguing picture of the Alpha and the Omega; all contribute to the formation of a rational basis for belief that something greater than the treasures of this life is offered to us.

Mysteries surround us today in science, in art, and in nature. Recently it was reported that a foundation granted $1.5 million to researchers in fields such as economics, oceanography, historical linguistics, computer science, population genetics, cell biology, and anthropology, to study the "unknowable." The president of the Sloan Foundation, which provided the funds, stated the reason for encouraging such research: "We are all taught what is known, but we rarely learn about what is not known, and we almost never learn about the unknowable."[1]

In science, we have questions raised by the unknown and the unseen, like primordial black holes, cold dark matter, and quantum particles. In computer science, philosophers and scientists continue to attempt to recreate the ability of human consciousness to understand and reason, to capture through artificial intelligence the elusive intuition and essence of human nature that is not yet understood.

In the arts we have the paradox of sublime music and pictures created by people who cannot, of themselves, provide explanation for the creation. Take for example the paradox of Mozart and his music. Mozart was perhaps the greatest composer who ever lived, but the clarity and brilliance of his music are completely contradicted by the disorder of his life and personality. Much of his sense of form and structure was clearly learned, but much of it appears to have been almost instinctive, reflecting an insight into beauty and human nature that was never apparent in his own personal life in any manner. The question that must be asked of Mozart is this: Can this music have arrived from a source other than the physical mind of the musician, a source that transcends our physical limitations?

In nature, mysteries abound. Consider one illustration, the dance of the honeybee. Scientists have discovered that when a honeybee locates a particular flower that contains a source of honey, it will return to report the discovery to the hive. The information is communicated through a strange but stylized geometric dance performed by the honeybee, which evidently traces a pattern providing exact directions to the source. The pattern implies the existence of more dimensions in space than we have experienced. How and why this happens is not understood; we just know that the dance is performed and the flower is identified by the swarm.[2]

These things provide the mystery—hints that there is more to the universe than we understand. They give us hints, but they don't really satisfy. After sifting through the evidence presented by science, the arts, nature, and the study of human consciousness in my search for truth, I have found that one source does exist to provide *direct* evidence for the existence of God and life after death—if the evidence sustains the assertions. That source is the testimony of four witnesses as set forth in the four books referred to as the Gospels of the New Testament. The core facts of the Gospel narratives are that a man named Jesus lived, died, and returned to life two thousand years ago. It is not necessary to examine each story in the Gospel narratives to find evidence of the existence of God and life after death. If only that testimony pertaining to the actual existence of Jesus, his death, and resurrection can be shown to be credible and believable under objective standards and the details can be corroborated, then proof of those unique events will necessarily provide a rational foundation for belief. The remainder of the message of the Gospels attains credibility from the truth of the resurrection.

In law, the key to proof of a case is the evidence—the stronger it is, the better the case. Direct testimony of an eyewitness is not required to prove a case; evidence of circumstances that combine to lead to a conclusion can also be very convincing. But testimony of an eyewitness who is found to be credible is extremely convincing, and the statements of two credible eyewitnesses that are consistent in material respects, if not expressly controverted, *require* belief. If the testimony of the Gospels represents credible eyewitness testimony, under the standards of the law it constitutes the strongest possible evidence.

In order to assure the integrity, or believability, of the evidence, however, it must meet certain tests of objectivity and verifiability. The same standards by which evidence is measured in a court of law can be applied to test the evidence offered in support of the truth of the Gospel testimony. Courts in the Western world have accepted the basic premise of the necessity for an objective standard and have therefore established rules governing the offer of evidence to prove a fact or an assertion. This book sets forth for the reader's consideration the evidence that is available to support a case for the testimony of the witnesses—Matthew, Mark, Luke, and John. That evidence is then tested to see if it would stand up in a court of law. It is not my purpose to diminish the rich message of the four Gospels or to reduce it to the shallowness of a few facts. But the life, death, and resurrection of Jesus, if they can be established to be historical fact under the rigorous standards of proof required in a court of law, provide us with a rational basis for belief in something beyond the physical world—the key to understanding the revelation and value of the full message.

If the testimony of the four Gospels can be established as true, then the value from that truth far exceeds the quicksilver melody of Mozart's music.

CHAPTER ONE

The Issue and the Standard of Proof

The life spirits of two small boys abandoned their bodies on a warm summer night in Texas in 1996. The children were five and six years old. A bloody nightshirt, a serrated bread knife, the wrong words spoken in a frantic telephone call to the police all led to the conviction of their mother for the murders. Darlie Routier was to all appearances a normal, loving person in the prime of her life. The cumulative impact of evidence, which was solely circumstantial, was enough to overcome an initial presumption of innocence in the case. Circumstantial evidence is the type of evidence that requires the use of reason to reach a conclusion. In the *Routier* case, no eyewitness ever appeared to support any portion of the prosecution's story, and yet she was convicted, sentenced to die by injection, and now waits on death row. Her family believes in her innocence; they maintain hope that somehow, some way, she can still be proven not guilty. The burden of proof has now shifted, however; without the introduction of new evidence, or the help of a technicality, she will face the executioner.[1]

Darlie Routier, like many others, was convicted solely on circumstantial evidence. Do you think that her family would still hold on to any hope if an eyewitness had testified at the trial? If a person of credible character, whose testimony was corroborated, appeared before the court to say, "I saw her kill them. I watched as she raised the knife over and over and stabbed each one with it"? What if two such witnesses appeared to so testify? In such a case, even with one eyewitness, surely with two, all hope of innocence would be extinguished for her husband, her mother, her friends. Testimony from a credible eyewitness is almost impossible to overcome.

The *Routier* case was built upon "knowable facts." This young mother would not be on death row if the case were built upon speculation or theories. The occurrence of an event such as murder is provable by putting together a case based upon evidence that is shown to be reliable in a court of law under objective standards provided to protect the integrity of the proof.

Today, in the gloaming of the twentieth century, we face a situation where knowable facts regarding an event so important that it could change each of our lives have been greatly obscured. The evidence that is available to support the truth of these facts is stronger than the evidence presented in the *Routier* case, stronger than that required to send a young woman to her death. And yet today, this evidence is being all but ignored.

The facts, if they are shown to be true, would establish that a person of human appearance, living on this earth, died and then came back to life—fully and completely. This is the cornerstone of the Christian religion. These facts have been ripped apart by theory and speculation, intellectually dissected to the effect that they are now generally believed to be based upon mythology, just stories to calm our fears, like a cup of chamomile tea. A message was sent to us, but the message has been discredited by sabotaging the messengers.

"Ah," you say, "a song of love and immortality. Such an amazing thing would require a lot of proof; no fallback to faith here, please." And what if you were to learn that these facts could be proven with authentic evidence of truthful eyewitness testimony, corroborated by investigative, forensic, and empirical evidence? Testimony that had first been scrubbed and polished by the limitations of the rules of evidence that are applicable for a test of truth in a federal court of law in the United States today? That would be a thing worthy of some consideration!

The prevailing twentieth-century school of thought ignores the evidence and posits that the entire foundation of the Christian religion is shifting sand, nothing more than mythology, that even the most fundamental portions of the New Testament are meaningless fiction. That Jesus, the man called Christ, was nothing more than a salesman, peddling his teachings from door to door, town to town, in self-aggrandizement naively accepted by gullible followers two thousand years ago. The consistent claim has been made by many of our intelligentsia that the Gospels, the four books of the New Testament that contain testimony to these facts, are merely stories that evolved over generations—under some theories over hundreds of years—after the time in which Jesus was alleged to have lived, written by unknown authors who built upon tradition, mythology, and a shred of teachings that have not been found but are speculated to exist. They assert that this was done possibly to create a political power base, or just a philosophy that overcame the shadow of the fear of death.

We are not required to accept one side of the issue or the other based upon theories or speculation, however. Since these are knowable facts, based upon the testimony of individual witnesses, they should be susceptible to proof. The evidence should be tested for authenticity and credibility against the same standards that apply in a court of law. Let us review, then, whether the manuscript evidence presented by these four Gospels would be admissible in a court of law in the United States today, and if we find that it is admissible, let us determine its credibility as evidence of the facts reported in the texts.

In the nineteenth century, Simon Greenleaf, a professor of law at Harvard University, wrote a treatise analyzing this very question. Simon Greenleaf was, and today remains, an established authority on the rules of evidence, having written a three-volume work on evidence, one of the most important works ever written on the law of evidence and one that is still used by lawyers in the United States. In the introduction to his treatise on the four Gospels, Greenleaf pointed out that this sort of investigation is a search for truth and error. It requires the reader to release himself or herself from existing prejudice; in other words, if you still hold preconceived, or *a priori,* convictions, you must set them aside in order to benefit from this analysis.

In our search for truth and error we will utilize the format of the original Greenleaf treatise as a basis for our analysis, but we will apply the current Federal Rules of Evidence and common law principles to the most recent facts and information available to us in the last decade of the twentieth century. Let us clear the smoke from our eyes and return to the simple facts.

What evidence is there to prove that the facts upon which the message of the Gospels depends are true? Archaeological, historical, and documentary evidence, scientific and medical evidence, evidence presented by the arts, evidence of statistical probabilities—all types of evidence exist to prove much more than a sufficient case that the testimony of the writers of the Gospels is true. If the events set forth in the Gospels can be shown to be actual historical facts, then the basic premise will have been established from which we can by reason infer that a personal God, not just an abstract ideal, also exists, and we can know that a continuing personal identity in life after death is real.

In order to determine the integrity of the evidence presented by the four Gospels, the review and analysis must be objective and thorough. The examination must be approached rationally. The evidence of the Gospels, notwithstanding its implications, should be judged by the same standards that are applied by law and science in all other situations. This book offers the supporting evidence gathered from many different expert witnesses for a conclusion that the message of the Gospels is truthful and reliable. Where it is necessary, opposing views have been presented, with a response if appropriate.

As the proponent of the proposition, I have assumed the burden of proof as an advocate for the truthfulness of the testimony of the Gospels. Each link in the chain of proof will be provided to you in detail in the format in which it would be presented if we were at trial in a courtroom, beginning with the basic question of the authenticity and admissibility of the documents in which the testimony is presented. The legal nature of the testimony—that is, whether it could be offered in court as eyewitness testimony and the credibility of that testimony—is examined. A summary and analysis of the evidence will thereafter be presented to you, because you, the reader, act as the jury. The summation includes a foundation for you to weigh the evidence and the probability that the conclusions in the summation are true or not true. I have tried to choose the best work of the experts in various fields to present for your consideration. Endnotes have been provided for reference to source material, and suggested reading has been included to assist you to go further in your own search if you are so inclined. Rules of evidence, whether statutory or derived from common law principles, will be placed in italics for identification.

To determine preliminarily what information would be admitted as evidence in a court of law, we begin with a rule of evidence used in federal courts in the United States today, which provides that all relevant evidence is admissible, unless it is otherwise excluded under those rules.[2] Evidence analyzed in accordance with the Federal Rules of Evidence is held to be relevant if it has the tendency to make the existence of the fact that you are trying to prove more probable, or less probable, than it would be without the evidence.[3] This is therefore a test of logical probability.

"Relevant evidence" means evidence having any tendency to make the existence of any fact that is of consequence to the determination of the action more

probable or less probable than it would be without the evidence.[4]

It is *facts* that establish the truth or falsity of the actual existence of Jesus and his crucifixion and resurrection. These fundamental facts are the foundation of Christianity, and they are subject to proof. The facts that we will try to prove through our analysis are set forth in the Gospels as testimony of witnesses who wrote those books, and therefore the credibility of the witnesses is at issue as well. The question to be answered is whether the witnesses themselves are entitled to belief. Are they credible? As you will see from the evidence, this is also susceptible to proof. For clarity we will repeat again the fundamental facts which underlie the issue of this case:

- Jesus lived approximately two thousand years ago
- Jesus died on the cross
- Jesus rose from the dead

The evidence that will be presented to you, the jury, will be limited to proof of the truth of the testimony of the four Gospels as to these particular facts, and no others.

The four Gospels satisfy the two components required of relevant evidence: The testimony is material and has probative value.[5] In other words, the Gospels are material to the case because they contain the statements of the very facts to be proved. The Gospels have probative value because, if the testimony itself is shown to be true, it will establish the truth of the facts. Direct evidence from a qualified witness that is offered in order to prove the facts at issue is never irrelevant.[6] As we have discussed, direct evidence is evidence that, if it is believed, resolves the issue. An example of this is the observation of an eyewitness, not otherwise controverted. In fact, the testimony of only one witness may be sufficient to prove a fact if you find that single witness believable.[7]

To prove the case, the jury will also be presented with circumstantial evidence. Proving a fact with circumstantial evidence requires proof of a chain of events, or facts from which the high probability of a conclusion may be deduced. Prosecutors in the *Routier* case illustrated how this works by summarizing the chain of circumstantial evidence against the defendant in their closing argument. Darlie Routier had claimed that an unknown assailant entered through a garage window at night, slashing open the screen, stabbing the two children first, then attacking her before leaving. The prosecution introduced a bread knife into evidence. It was found neatly stored in a kitchen knife holder. Tiny pieces of fiberglass and rubber were found on the knife by use of a powerful microscope. The materials on the knife were identical to components of the slashed window screen. Strong traces of blood were found on the sink and faucet, as if blood had been washed from the knife. It was determined that the knife was in fact the murder weapon, and no other weapon was ever found.

Additionally, the nightshirt that Darlie was wearing had splatters of blood on the back, consistent with leaning over her sleeping sons to stab them, then raising the knife over her shoulder to repeat the action but inconsistent with her own story. The wounds were deep, but Darlie, the potential remaining witness, was only wounded superficially; contrary to testimony by expert witnesses that this contradicted patterns established in past murder cases where witnesses, particularly adult witnesses, were not left alive.[8]

The cumulative effect of the evidence in the *Routier* case

was powerful proof of the murder charge. This evidence is circumstantial—evidence of the circumstances—and it leads us to the highest degree of probability of this person's guilt. It is strong enough to prove the fact in a court of law, strong enough to cause this young mother to face the death penalty. The circumstantial evidence that will be presented to the jury to prove the facts at issue in this case and the credibility of the testimony of the Gospel witnesses is of the same nature.

Our opponents who deny the truth of the Gospel testimony—opposing counsel—have presented that case to the public for the last 150 years, and the jury is invited to weigh the evidence against that yardstick as well. Cross-examinations have also been provided to the jury in this case in specific instances concerning facts that have been most prominently disputed.

The implications that flow from the facts before the jury will not be addressed during the presentation of evidence other than to the extent that an understanding of the scientific cause of certain events bears on credibility of the testimony. The facts to be proved should be judged on their own by the same standards applied to facts proposed in any other civil case presented in a federal court in the United States, without consideration in advance of the conclusion.

At the end of our "trial," you, the jury, will be asked to render a verdict based upon a preponderance of the evidence. This means that you must consider all of the evidence that has been presented to you and determine whether you are persuaded that the testimony of the Gospels—that Jesus lived two thousand years ago, died on the cross, and came back to life—is *more likely than not* to be true. This is the standard of proof ordinarily required for a civil case presented in a federal court.[9]

It is important in this type of legal analysis not to let a philosophical commitment to a certain conclusion, a predisposition, interfere with your objective examination of observable data and solid evidence, direct or circumstantial. Beware the temptation to reject or ignore in advance data that appear to be leading to a conclusion that you think will make you uncomfortable. You may think that this is an unnecessary warning, but you would be surprised at the number of brilliant thinkers in the world who have made this very basic mistake. Albert Einstein made the greatest mistake of his scientific career when he realized that his general theory of relativity provided evidence of an expanding universe that implied that the universe had a beginning and an end. Because a beginning requires a "beginner," Einstein fudged his equations to avoid that conclusion. The correction factor inserted by Einstein was proven wrong by the astronomer Edwin Hubble some years later, leading to the "big bang" theory of the creation of the universe. Current studies in astrophysics have determined that Einstein may indeed have been on to something—but for the wrong reasons.[10]

So now . . . let the courtroom be illuminated. You are seated in the jury box to hear the case—that two thousand years ago a man named Jesus lived, died, and returned to life in human form. Let us examine the testimony of four people who lived at that time and reported that these events actually occurred, and then you will weigh the evidence and determine if these reports are more likely than not to be true.

CHAPTER TWO

Admissibility and Authentication of the Evidence

As you enter the jury box you will notice that you have become the center of attention. As a juror you are told a story, and, because you will render the verdict, you become a part of the story—each piece of evidence is presented especially to you in order to create a cumulative effect that is connected and convincing. But your universe within which the story is created is limited; you will only be permitted to hear and consider evidence which is admissible—that is, evidence that meets certain standards developed over hundreds of years. This is the system that is used in the courtroom to regulate evidence offered to prove a case. Some of these standards have been solidified as rules, referred to as the Federal Rules of Evidence. Others have evolved as principles carved from a composite of experiences over the centuries, as a diamond is cut from the stone. These are referred to as common law principles.

By the time the jury begins to hear the story, the question of whether the evidence to be presented is admissible for consideration has usually already been decided by the judge. In our case, however, we will begin at the beginning because scholars fond of the chamomile tea theory of religion—or opposing counsel—have claimed generally that the four Gospels of the New Testament constitute a form of evidence that is, by legal standards, weak. The presumption has been made that the testimony of the writers of the Gospels is of no great weight because it would be dismissed as hearsay evidence if subjected to scrutiny in a court of law. This is incorrect.

Let us therefore first examine whether the documentary evidence presented by these four Gospels would be admissible in a court of law in the United States today, and, if admissible, would be credible as evidence of the facts reported in the texts. The evidence that we will examine begins with handwritten manuscripts containing the earliest dated copies of the complete Gospels in the New Testament, as well as many fragments of early manuscripts of the Gospels written on material produced from papyrus, a tall aquatic plant. These fragments are sometimes referred to collectively as "papyri."

No original manuscripts of the four Gospels are in existence; we will be dealing with some of the earliest copies, however. The importance of the fragments is to establish early dates for the actual writing of the original manuscripts, and this process will be made clear below.

The oldest manuscript in existence of all four Gospels and

the Book of Acts dates from the first quarter of the third century, although it is believed by many scholars to be much older. Part of this manuscript is held at Chester Beatty Library in Dublin; and the other part resides at the Austrian National Library in Vienna. We will refer to this from now on as the Chester Beatty manuscript.

The Vatican owns the earliest substantially complete manuscript of the entire New Testament, which is dated to approximately A.D. 325. This manuscript, known as the Codex Vaticanus, appears of record in 1475 in the first catalog of the Vatican Library. It has been strictly guarded by Vatican security since that time. Scholars hold the Codex Vaticanus to be one of the most trustworthy copies of the original texts of the New Testament.[1]

The next earliest substantially complete manuscript of the entire New Testament, including the Gospels, is the Codex Sinaiticus, written in approximately A.D. 350.[2] This manuscript is currently held by the British Museum in London. Constantin Tischendorf discovered the mildewed, weathered pages of the Codex Sinaiticus lying unprotected in baskets at a monastery at the foot of Mount Sinai in 1844. The monks of the monastery had not appreciated the value of the manuscripts and had already burned a great bulk of them for heat. What remained is believed to have survived because the monastery was located in a remote region and thus protected from invasions over the years. This manuscript is generally also held to be an early and reliable copy of the original New Testament manuscripts.[3]

In addition to the substantially complete manuscripts of the New Testament described above, thousands of other ancient handwritten manuscripts of the New Testament, including more than five thousand Greek manuscripts, as well as approximately one hundred papyrus fragments from all of the twenty-seven books of the New Testament, are currently held in museums and libraries throughout the world.[4]

We have seen that the Gospel manuscripts are relevant evidence; however, that determination does not cause them to be automatically admissible for the jury's consideration. These Gospel manuscripts contain statements by witnesses, or declarants, who are not available at this time in court for cross-examination in front of the jury. Preliminarily under the general rule, if such out-of-court statements are offered as truth of the facts they assert, they would ordinarily be excluded as hearsay evidence.[5] The ideal conditions for a witness to testify are that the witness is under oath, personally present at the trial, and subject to cross-examination. Nevertheless, an exception is permitted under the law for statements contained in an "ancient document," and the Gospel manuscripts fall within that exception. For legal purposes these manuscripts and the papyrus fragments will be permitted as evidence in a court of law if they can be authenticated as true ancient documents, that is, if they meet the following tests:

> *An ancient document will be admissible as evidence in a court of law if its authenticity is established.*[6]

> *The requirement of authentication or identification as a condition precedent to admissibility for an ancient document is satisfied with evidence that the document, in any form (A) is in such condition as to create no suspicion concerning its authenticity, (B) was in a place where it, if authentic, would likely be,*

*and (C) has been in existence twenty years or more
at the time it is offered as evidence.*[7]

Authentication of the manuscripts or documents presented
will establish the genuineness of the manuscripts as being what
they purport to be—in this case, a report of certain events
observed by the writers. Courts have recognized the necessity of
admitting ancient documents as evidence for consideration by
the jury, even though the assertions in the documents constitute
statements made by witnesses who are not actually present in
the courtroom, because of the passage of time since the events
reported in the documents and the difficulty of producing other
similar evidence. Once authenticated, the four Gospels will be
admissible as evidence for the jury's consideration.

Under our legal system it is thought that the age of the
manuscript provides assurance that the writing clearly predates
the controversy at issue; that is one of the rationales underlying
the exception to the hearsay rule. Additionally, error is mini-
mized because this exception applies only to written statements.
This protects against the risk of error in the transmission of
oral statements, for example, removal of the statement from the
actual context in which it was made.[8] As you will see, the age
of the manuscript is important when making a judgment as to
the *credibility* of this evidence as well.

If the document is authenticated properly, the testimony of
the ancient document is usually considered to have been
removed from any incentive to lie or invent the facts reported.
Let us acknowledge in advance, however, that the issue of
whether the writers of the Gospels actually had any motive or
incentive to falsify the testimony in the document must be
explored further. This analysis is also proper in the context of

examining the credibility of the evidence. A motive or incentive to fabricate the testimony would of course have an impact on the weight that the jury would give to the evidence.

In answer to the question of motive to falsify, history teaches that the authors wrote their Gospels at a time when they had absolutely no incentive to be dishonest in relating the events they narrated. It is a historical fact that it was politically and socially dangerous to preach the gospel in Palestine, Rome, or the surrounding areas in the first century. Even if it were possible to deceive so many people into believing that Jesus had risen from his grave three days after burial, the witnesses would have had great incentive to conclude that this was not true. The authors of the Gospels certainly had nothing to gain materially or politically from telling the stories. All of them suffered greatly for the rest of their lives, and most of them died as a result of their belief that this resurrection occurred. For example, in A.D. 115 Ignatius, a bishop in the early Christian church in Antioch, Syria, wrote that as a result of persecution for their beliefs, "Peter was crucified, Paul and James were slain with the sword; John was banished to [the island of] Patmos; Stephen was stoned to death . . ."[9]

The danger inherent in the position of the authors of the Gospels or that of any other person preaching the word of the Gospels in the first century is evident in the historically verified treatment of that group of people. In A.D. 37 the mad Caligula became emperor of Rome, and worship of any god in preference to him was an invitation to cruel oppression. Any reference to Jesus as the "Messiah" or with an indication of divinity or even kingship was inflammatory. Caligula was replaced by Claudius in A.D. 41, and followers of Jesus were temporarily expelled from Rome because they were viewed as troublemakers—as a monotheistic group they refused to recognize the emperor as god.[10] Agrippa I, a grandchild of Herod the Great, became the client-king of Judea under Caligula and continued to reign under Claudius. As members of a messianic movement disliked by both the Jewish leadership and the Romans, Christians became an attractive target for Agrippa.[11] The followers of Jesus were isolated. Their situation became precarious, from everyday economic deprivation to the terror of relentless persecution.

In A.D. 67 the emperor Nero treated the people of Rome to a great circus of events, using Christians as the entertainment. The early writer Tacitus described it this way: "Besides being put to death they were made to serve as objects of amusement; they were clad in the hides of beasts and torn to death by dogs; others were crucified, others set on fire to serve to illuminate the night when daylight failed. Nero had thrown open his grounds for the display, and was putting on a show in the circus, where he mingled with the people in the dress of a charioteer or drove about in his chariot."[12] Tacitus lived between A.D. 55 and 117 and was known to have hated both Christians and Jews alike. He referred to Christians as "a class hated for their abominations."[13]

A letter from Pliny (the Younger), governor of Bithynia, in what is now known as Turkey, to the emperor Trajan during the same period, made it clear that in general a follower of the teachings of Jesus could escape punishment easily by recanting his or her belief in Christianity.[14] He described his method of interrogation: "I ask them if they are Christians. If they admit it I repeat the question a second and third time, threatening capital punishment; if they persist, I sentence them to death. For I do not doubt that, whatever kind of crime it may be to which they have confessed, their pertinacity and inflexible obstinacy should certainly be punished. . . . All who denied that they were or had been Christians I considered should be discharged . . ."[15]

A picture of the prison in Rome known as the Mamertine in which many followers of Jesus died and in which the apostle Peter is believed to have been held for nine months illustrates what awaited anyone who held to the belief that Jesus rose from the dead. The Mamertine was a dungeon, described as a dank underground hole cut out of surrounding rock, with only two ten-foot-deep chambers. Prisoners were thrown into the hole through one entrance in the ceiling. No fresh air or light could enter, and it was never cleaned. Prisoners went mad in this dungeon; almost everyone who entered the Mamertine died there.[16]

The historical facts do not support an argument that a reasonable motive existed for falsification of the Gospel testimony. We may therefore assume, unless otherwise contradictory evidence comes to light, that the authors of the Gospels had no motive for fabrication, and that the rationale underlying the exception for ancient documents holds true for introduction of the Gospels as evidence.

Under the rule of evidence recited above, for purposes of authentication, the documents must first be shown to be free of suspicion concerning authenticity. A document produced from proper custody is free from suspicion unless it bears marks of forgery, or appears otherwise clearly unreliable on its face, for example, if the flow of content is inconsistent. Bruce Metzger, a highly regarded authority on the textual integrity of the New

Testament manuscripts, has stated that "the fact is that in most manuscripts the size of the letters and the ductus of the script remain surprisingly uniform throughout even lengthy documents."[17] Because of the age of these manuscripts, portions are missing from some of them. But the existing manuscripts show a high degree of care in preparation. For example, the Codex Sinaiticus shows that it was carefully executed, and before it was permitted to leave the scriptorium, it was checked and corrected by scribes, known as "correctors," who designated each correction with individual signs of identification.[18]

The rule deals only with the authentication of the document that is to be proved. However, it does not go to the actual content of the document but rather to whether the document is in fact what it purports to be. Questions as to its content and completeness really bear upon the weight that the jury will give to the evidence, but these do not affect the threshold question of authenticity.[19] The Gospel manuscripts and the relevant papyrus fragments bear no demonstrations of forgery or other unreliability. The precision with which these documents have been authenticated over the years by the Christian church, which will be described in detail below, establishes the reliability of the manuscripts. Furthermore, they bear no evidence of having been prepared in anticipation of controversy.

The second question to be examined to determine if these documents will be admissible as evidence over a hearsay objection is whether the documents were found in a place where such a writing might naturally and reasonably be expected to be found.[20] If so, the court will examine whether they were maintained by, and held in the care of, persons whom you would expect to have custody of them.

Applying the law to the facts of the case, we must consider that these manuscripts, as well as other portions of the New Testament, have not only been held in the custody of and used in the Christian church for almost two thousand years, but they have been examined for authenticity numerous times, not only by Christian scholars but also by critics. This test of authenticity was applicable under Greenleaf's analysis even in the nineteenth century, before the Federal Rules of Evidence were enacted. Greenleaf concluded that the Gospel manuscripts were found where they would be expected to have been found, and their custodians were those whom one would expect to care for them. Customarily they have been treated as sacred writings by their custodians and have been treated as the plain narratives of the writers. There is no assertion made by any custodian of the manuscripts that the originals were derived in any unusual or miraculous manner. Additionally, the documents were made public at the time they were written; that they were not held secretly has been well documented not only by early Christian writers and scholars but also by general historians.

Third, to comply with the twenty-year requirement for authentication of an ancient document, the age of the writing may be shown by testimony of expert witnesses, or witnesses with knowledge, that the documents have been held in the possession of another person or institution for over twenty years; or age may be determined by the physical appearance of the manuscript, or even by the contents itself, taken with the surrounding circumstances. Additionally, the age of a document can be identified by an expert witness from analysis of the paper, ink, handwriting, and through scientific tests, by comparisons to other documents that have been authenticated, or by analysis of other marks or indicia on the paper.[21] Clearly the Gospel manuscripts described earlier, and the papyrus fragments, satisfy the age requirement. Extensive evidence of the age of the manuscripts and the papyri will be offered to the jury in the following chapters when we examine the legal nature of the Gospels and the credibility of that testimony.

A statement in a document that is at least twenty years old and whose authenticity has been established in accordance with the preceding requirements may be admitted as evidence of the truth of the facts that are recited in the statement.[22] The fact that is established by authentication is the truth of the assertions made by the writers of the Gospels that the things they saw occurred, and the words they heard were spoken. For example, if Jane Jones testifies that she heard John Smith say that a ball was red, the fact established is that Jane Jones actually heard John Smith make that statement, not that the ball was actually red. Similarly, if the apostle John testified that he personally observed Jesus alive after his death on the cross, the fact to be established is whether John observed that event, *not* the underlying implications of those facts.

An interesting case provides an illustration of this legal principle. In 1857 a vessel left the port of Havana for New York, carrying more than six hundred passengers and $2 million in gold. Off the coast of South Carolina it sailed into the full fury of a hurricane. Most of the passengers and all of the gold were lost at sea.[23] Of course, news of the great tragedy was reported all over the world. After decades of searching for the ship, in 1987 it was found and a contest over the ownership of the salvage ensued. In court, insurance companies argued that they owned the gold because they had paid the insurance claims in 1857. The insurance companies had no copies of the policies, no copies of invoices, no proof of loss or any other records. Under the ancient documents exception to the hearsay rule, the court permitted introduction of the old newspaper articles to prove that the gold was in fact insured by these companies. The facts of the tragedy contained in the articles were accepted as true, but the companies still had to prove the rest of their case.[24]

Some courts will require the proponent of the evidence, that is, the person making the assertion, to show that the witnesses had an adequate opportunity to observe the facts reported. Because of the age of the ancient writing, in the process of authentication courts generally will not require proof that the author of the text actually had personal knowledge of the event, but will probably require a showing from the circumstances that the witness *had the opportunity to have obtained* personal knowledge of the event.[25] After such a lapse of time it would be unreasonable to require strict proof that the declarant personally observed the facts recorded. The practical approach has been to review the circumstances to determine whether the declarant *could have had* personal knowledge of the matters recited. If it is determined that the declarant could not have had personal knowledge about the events, the recitals in the documents might not be accepted as true statements of what the witness saw or heard.[26] The legal nature of the testimony of the Gospels—that is, whether they represent eyewitness testimony—will be examined extensively in the next chapter. Preliminarily, however, new evidence shows that the Gospels were written at a date sufficiently early to establish that the authors could have been present at the events that occurred.

One of the reasons that we have limited the issue in this case solely to the truth of the reports of the life, death, and resurrection of Jesus is to simplify the process of proof by limiting that proof to statements of the core facts upon which Christianity is based, facts that the authors of the Gospels had the personal opportunity to observe and know. An attempt to prove that each story or statement reported in the Gospels occurred would require us to test each such event separately against the hearsay rule and the other rules of evidence, a process beyond the necessary scope of the present work.

Thus, we have seen that the Gospels are documents of the requisite age, coming from the proper custody, and free of suspicious appearances. They meet all of the requirements for authentication under the rules of evidence. Once documents, such as the Gospel manuscripts and the papyrus fragments, qualify as ancient documents, they will be excepted from the limitations of the hearsay rule.[27]

At the time that the original Gospels were written, most writing was on papyrus paper, which was easily destroyed. The Chester Beatty manuscript is written on papyrus. The Codex Sinaiticus and Codex Vaticanus are written on vellum (sometimes also referred to as parchment), which is made from the skins of certain animals that have been especially prepared. It is clear that the manuscripts Codex Sinaiticus and Codex Vaticanus, as well as the Chester Beatty manuscripts, are copies and not the original manuscripts. Although the best evidence is required to be offered, the original document is not required to be produced for comparison if all originals are lost or have been destroyed, unless the person introducing the evidence lost or destroyed them in bad faith.[28]

A duplicate is admissible to the same extent as an
original unless (1) a genuine question is raised as to
the authenticity of the original, or (2) in the circum-
stances it would be unfair to admit the duplicate in
lieu of the original.[29]

The copied manuscripts and the papyrus fragments are therefore admissible as evidence to the same extent as the originals.
The process of authentication of a copy of the original manuscript is the same as that set forth for an original.[30]

The copies are highly reliable. The copying of manuscripts
in the first century was an important task, and it was performed by hand with great precision. Thousands of copies of
the original manuscripts of the Gospels were made in the first
centuries after the death of Jesus. The empirical findings of
papyrology have matched papyrus fragments of the early dated
manuscripts word for word in comparison with the corresponding texts in the later complete manuscripts. The science of papyrology identifies and dates all ancient texts other than inscriptions, and it includes such related disciplines as paleography, the
study of handwriting. The integrity of the later copies has been
verified by these comparisons.

Comparisons have also been made between the accuracy of
the newer handwritten complete manuscript texts of the New
Testament containing the four Gospels and the earliest versions
of those documents, including the papyri, and the copies have
been held to be much more accurate than copies preserved of
other ancient writings. Rules governing the integrity of the copying of these manuscripts were strictly enforced, and severe penal-
ties were imposed for carelessness.[31] The differences, or textual
variations, between later manuscripts and the earliest complete

manuscripts, as well as the early complete manuscripts and the even earlier papyri fragments, have been found to be negligible.

In addition, the integrity of the manuscripts can be tested not only against each other, but also against independent quotations taken from the oldest copies of the New Testament books, including the Gospels. Writings of early church fathers in the second and third centuries A.D. contain more than thirty-six thousand quotations from verses of the New Testament. In fact, with the exception of only eleven verses, it has been said that the entire New Testament could be reconstructed today from those writings even if we had no actual manuscripts.[32]

The textual integrity of the New Testament is much more reliable than that of other ancient documents. For example, there are 643 manuscript copies of the *Iliad* in existence and they are similar in length to the New Testament. While only about 40 lines of the New Testament have been questioned, 764 lines of the *Iliad* are questioned. Scholars who have made these comparisons have concluded that the New Testament is textually purer than any other great book.[33]

Of the variations among the early and later handwritten copies of the manuscripts found in the New Testament, only a slight number of the variants have been found to have any weight, and most of them are merely mechanical matters such as spelling or style. A study of the textual variants in the existing New Testament manuscripts can be somewhat confusing because if one word is misspelled in three thousand different manuscripts, textual critics will count this as three thousand variants rather than one. After adjusting for that procedure however, it has been estimated that the degree of substantial purity of extant texts of the New Testament is 98 to 99 percent.[34] F. F. Bruce, a well-known biblical scholar, has stated that textual critics of the New Testament have found no variants that affect material questions of historical fact or belief upon which Christianity is founded.[35] Sir Frederick Kenyon has stated that "not one fundamental doctrine of the Christian faith rests on a disputed reading," a statement again recently verified by Philip Comfort.[36]

Most of the scribes responsible for making copies of the Gospels were Jews with a background of great respect for religious teaching and writing. Strict rules governed the work of the scribes, whether the books were viewed as sacred Scripture or literary works. The four Gospels, however, are believed to have been treated as sacred books from the beginning.[37] Established patterns required to be followed by Jewish scribes copying Old Testament Scriptures are evident in the manuscripts that were copied for what is now known as the New Testament. For example, special abbreviations designating holy names are found in both New and Old Testament manuscripts. The New Testament papyri and manuscripts have been found to have been produced with extreme care by educated and professional scribes, many influenced by the methods of scholarship required for work in the scriptorium for the library at Alexandria in Egypt.[38]

Although a study of the Old Testament is not our purpose, it is relevant to consider the Dead Sea Scrolls, found at the caves of Qumran in 1946, to appreciate the accuracy and precision with which ancient texts were transmitted. Until that time a Hebrew manuscript known as the Aleppo Codex was the oldest known manuscript containing the full text of the entire Bible. It was written in Israel in about A.D. 900. The books of the Old Testament found in the Dead Sea Scrolls written approximately one thousand years before the Aleppo Codex were found to be almost identical to those of the Aleppo Codex. For example, in the scrolls found in the caves at Qumran was a manuscript of the Book of Isaiah, dated about 200 B.C. Scholars were amazed to find only thirteen minor variations between the Book of Isaiah contained in the Aleppo Codex and the Book of Isaiah found in the Dead Sea Scrolls.[39]

Even modern versions of the Bible, with the possible exception of new thought-for-thought translations, evidence few variants from original texts. An example of this is shown by a fragment of a scroll written on beaten silver. This fragment, held in Jerusalem, is known as the "silver scroll."[40] Dating between 700 and 500 B.C., the silver scroll was found in 1981 in a gravesite in Jerusalem. In microscopic handwriting, this fragment contains words from the Old Testament Book of Numbers:

"The Lord bless you and keep you;
The Lord make His face shine on you,
And be gracious to you;
The Lord lift up His countenance on you,
And give you peace." (Num. 6:24–25)

The words are virtually identical to modern texts. This is an example of the "amazing fidelity of transmission" throughout a period of over twenty-five hundred years by generations of scribes responsible for making manuscript copies of the Old and New Testaments of the Bible.

It is also important to recognize that at the time that copies of the original manuscripts of the four Gospels began to be created and circulated in the first century, the great interest of the Christian communities in the accurate preservation of the original language provided a natural monitor for the work of the scribes. The original manuscripts appear to have recorded oral teachings that were themselves public. It was well known that copies of the original manuscripts, incorporating the public teachings, were being made and circulated. The manuscripts themselves contain recitals of events that were not only of great interest to the general public at the time, but they also described events which happened in front of many witnesses. Inaccuracies in the manuscripts would have been subject to public criticism. Since no such contemporary criticism is of record, it can reasonably be assumed that the testimony in the manuscripts represented the consensus of the community.

Because of the public interest in these documents, Greenleaf concluded in his nineteenth-century treatise that the scribes will be regarded for legal purposes as the agents of the Christian communities, for whose use the copies were made. Copies made under these circumstances would be given great confidence in a court of law as evidence and would be *presumed* to be true copies until proven otherwise. This is particularly compelling, given the fact that these four Gospels have been universally accepted as true copies of the original narratives and have been consistently acted upon by the Christian community throughout the last two thousand years.[41]

The early manuscript copies of the four Gospels, together with the papyrus fragments, have now been authenticated and constitute relevant evidence that is fully admissible in a federal court of law. They are sufficient under the Federal Rules of Evidence and applicable common law for consideration by the jury in judging the truth or falsity of the facts that we have set out to examine and prove.

CHAPTER THREE

The Legal Nature of the Testimony

H aving determined that the early manuscript copies that form the basis of the evidence presented by the Gospels are admissible as evidence for consideration by the jury, the legal nature of these four writings must be clarified. This will be one of the factors to be weighed by the jury in forming the verdict. We must ascertain who wrote them and how we know that. The identity of the writers must be examined, and thereafter the credibility of the authors of the Gospels as witnesses describing these events must be established. This will require a review not only of the testimony set forth in the actual manuscripts, but also of the corroborating evidence provided by archaeology, other sciences such as papyrology, and historical writings.

In an examination of the legal nature of these four writings, we will review first the relationship of the authors to the events reported. Are these reports presented as testimony of knowledgeable and credible witnesses? The authorship of the Gospels is a subject that has been studied continuously since the first century because the historical truth of the writings is the very foundation of the Christian religion. This analysis will help us to discover whether each writer was in a position to have actually observed the events recorded. That is significant because, even though the Gospels as we have now authenticated them will be admitted as evidence over the hearsay objection, the normal requirement that a witness giving testimony should have firsthand knowledge remains an important standard for determining the credibility, or the actual value, that the jury will give to that testimony. If the testimony is not based upon personal observation, it will have to satisfy some other exception from the rule to be viewed as credible. The basic requirement is this:

> *A witness may not testify to a matter unless evidence*
> *is introduced sufficient to support a finding that the*
> *witness has personal knowledge of the matter.*
> *Evidence to prove personal knowledge may, but need*
> *not, consist of the witness' own testimony.*[1]

Federal Rule of Evidence 602, quoted above, has been interpreted by courts with some flexibility to permit either a showing of firsthand knowledge, or alternatively, a showing that circumstances were "sufficient to support a finding" that the witness had firsthand knowledge of the facts reported.[2] In other words, if circumstances surrounding the facts lead you to conclude that the author had the opportunity to observe the events, for example, that he or she lived at that time and in that geographical place, and other evidence appears to corroborate personal observation, that is generally sufficient to meet the requirements of the rule. Courts have ruled that such things as evidence of a person's lengthy experience with the subject,[3] expertise on a subject, and personal background;[4] inferences customarily drawn from particular circumstances or procedures;[5] and knowledge obtained from some acceptable source, such as a photograph,[6] are all sufficient to meet the requirements of the rule in place of actual proof of firsthand observation. In a situation in which the evidence that the witness had an adequate opportunity to observe the facts is uncertain, the evidence will be admitted and the jury will decide the issue.

The question of whether the Gospels were written by witnesses who had personal knowledge—or who had the opportunity to have personal knowledge—of the events reported depends in large part upon the date that can be assigned to the earliest manuscripts containing testimony of those facts. As you know, the challenge is that the Gospels are not eyewitness testimony, but merely myths and legends, in some cases reflecting tradition or political agenda, that arose gradually over a long period following the death of Jesus. This view is essentially based upon a primary assumption that the Gospels themselves were not actually written in complete form until several generations after the death of Jesus—at the earliest, near the end of the first century.[7]

Scholars have spent entire careers dating the earliest manuscripts of the New Testament and, more recently, the papyrus fragments. To begin to create the time frame for dating, we know that the earliest date for the Gospels is the year of the crucifixion of Jesus, commonly accepted to be between A.D. 30 and 33. Dating by comparison to texts with a known end-date because they refer to a specific event is sometimes also possible. For example, a manuscript discovered within the caves at Qumran, known as the Dead Sea Scrolls, would have an outside date of A.D. 68, the year when the caves were abandoned as the inhabitants fled before an invasion of the Tenth Roman Legion. That end-date for the Dead Sea Scrolls was also confirmed by radiocarbon dating in 1991.[8]

The invasion of Roman soldiers mentioned above foretold one of the most important events in Jewish history, and it provides another possible end-date for the Gospel manuscripts. In A.D. 68 the drumbeat of Rome reverberated throughout Palestine as the soldiers of Nero's general Titus marched to Jerusalem. After a long siege the city was completely sealed off from the outside world. The Romans built a massive wall of earth around Jerusalem and famine soon conquered the inhabitants. Jerusalem was destroyed, sacked, and burned to the ground in A.D. 70. The Jewish historian Flavius Josephus, born circa A.D. 37, wrote *Wars of the Jews* in A.D. 77 or 78, and thereafter a monumental history called *Antiquities of the Jews*. He described the wrath of the Romans as they nailed the Jews upon crosses in front of the walls of the city, "one after one way, and another after another, to the crosses, by way of jest; when their multitude was so great, that room was wanting for the crosses, and crosses wanting for the bodies."[9]

When the Romans entered the city, they found streets and houses full of dying women, children, and elderly people, "and the young men wandered about the market-places like shadows, all swelled with famine. . . ."[10] The city was plundered. Blood and fire dominated the landscape. The temple was destroyed in the conflagration and with it the entire institutional system of Judaism that was centered on the temple. Josephus reports that so many children, old men, profane persons, and priests were slain that the ground beneath them was no longer visible. Desolation reigned throughout Judea. Every historical writing from A.D. 70 through the second century reflected this dramatic circumstance—the change in the Jewish system and its relationship with Rome—except the four Gospels.

The silence of the Gospels with respect to the destruction of Jerusalem and the temple is strong circumstantial evidence that they were written before, not after, A.D. 70. The Gospels reflect the social, cultural, and economic background of the period prior to the destruction of Jerusalem and the Jewish Levitical system, not after. They reflect a delicate but still tolerable relationship with Rome, not the hostile servility of a nation enslaved and broken. Logic does not permit a conclusion that the Gospels could have been written after the year A.D. 70 without mention of the Jewish revolt and the resulting destruction of the city, the temple, the Jewish culture, and the new hostility with Rome. That reasoning alone provides a rational basis for belief by many knowledgeable scholars that A.D. 70 should be viewed as an end-date for the writing of the Gospels.

In addition to the end-date of A.D. 70, internal references in the narratives of the various Gospels, and perhaps more important, silence as to other major historical events, provide further evidence of an early date. The Gospels contain no hint of the persecution of Christians by Nero in A.D. 67, even though the facts were well known and Tacitus stated that the excesses of that period gained great public sympathy for the victims at the time.[11] Neither do any of the Gospels contain a reference to the stoning death of James, the brother of Jesus and a leader of the early Christian church, at approximately the same time, though that event was reported by Josephus in his *Antiquities of the Jews*.[12] The Gospels do not contain any reference to the death of the apostle Peter or of Paul, another follower of Jesus after his crucifixion.

On the other hand, the Gospels affirmatively reflect the need to distinguish the new message of Jesus from Jewish law as it existed prior to A.D. 70 on such subjects as fasting, the relationship to the temple, and the requirement of sacrifices, all of which disappeared after the destruction of Jerusalem. John A. T. Robinson, a well-known biblical scholar, has given the example, among others, that the Gospel of Matthew seven times warns against the influence of the Sadducees, a group whose power totally disappeared after the destruction of the temple. The Gospel of Matthew also reflects a continued need to coexist with a Jewish culture that was no longer in existence after the destruction of the temple in A.D. 70.[13] Historians have recognized that after A.D. 70, Christians and Jews separated into two completely different camps, and that fact is reflected in many Jewish and Christian writings. Based upon this reasoning, the situation described in the Gospels corresponds to what is known about Christianity in Palestine prior to A.D. 70.[14]

The facts and analysis described above are completely inconsistent with a theory that the Gospels were written at or near the end of the first century or in the early second century. Reason requires a date prior to A.D. 70 for the writing of the four Gospels on that basis alone. Additionally, through corroboration of the incidental details of all of the Gospel narratives, recent archaeological discoveries that will be presented to the jury also support a very early date for the four Gospels. Robinson believed, based on the foregoing reasoning, that all the Gospels were completed during the forty years that passed between the death of Jesus and the destruction of Jerusalem.[15]

New forensic evidence of an even earlier date for some of the Gospels has recently been announced, however, further eroding the theory that the four Gospels were written at a date too late to permit the authors to have been alive at the time of the events reported. This has been described as the most stunning breakthrough in biblical research since the discovery of the Dead Sea Scrolls! Papyrus fragments of the Gospel of Matthew, and possibly those of the Gospels of Mark and Luke and the New Testament Book of Acts, can now be shown to have been written by people of the same generation as Jesus—people who were alive at the time that Jesus lived. These fragments containing random selections from the Gospels have recently been matched word for word against the related portions of the later complete manuscripts of those books, providing evidence not only of the early date of those Gospels, but also that the actual Gospels *in their entirety* were written at the earlier dates.[16]

The recent redating of three papyrus fragments containing Greek script from the twenty-sixth chapter of the Gospel of Matthew provides a starting point for an examination of this evidence and a watershed for reassessment of the dates of the original authorship of the four Gospels. These three fragments were acquired at Luxor, Egypt, by the Reverend Charles Huleatt and were donated to Magdalen College, Oxford, in 1901. Known as the "Magdalen fragments," they appear to come from a codex, not a scroll, since the script appears on both sides of the papyrus.[17] In 1994 Carsten Thiede, a papyrologist and director of the Institute for Basic Epistemological Research in Paderborn, Germany, saw the fragments for the first time and was perplexed at the second-century date that had been assigned to them. He began a full study and analysis of the Magdalen fragments that resulted in an assignment of a new early date for the Gospel of Matthew.

The Magdalen fragments contain a description from the twenty-sixth chapter of Matthew of the anointing of Jesus in the house of Simon the leper at Bethany, his betrayal to the chief priests by Judas Iscariot, Judas's negotiations with the chief priests for the price of Jesus, the Last Supper, and the promise of Jesus to return after his death. The fragments contain not only the words of Jesus but also the narrative and words of others, such as Judas.[18] Thiede has also concluded that related fragments from an earlier portion of the Gospel of Matthew that are held in Barcelona are probably from the same codex.[19] These Barcelona fragments describe the meeting of John the Baptist and Jesus and the Sermon on the Mount. Thiede has now reported that the three Magdalen fragments were dated circa A.D. 66 at the *latest,* within thirty-three to thirty-six years of the death of Jesus. Because they were already in wide circulation at that time, however, an earlier date is probable.

Dating of manuscripts, or a fragment of a manuscript, is accomplished in various ways. The papyrus fragments of the Gospel manuscripts cannot be tested by radiocarbon dating because they are too small and too light. Thiede concluded that even the new technology of accelerator mass spectrometry was unavailable because the fragments are so light that there would be danger of their being destroyed in the process. Because the letters extend to the edges of the fragments, it is not even possible to separate a piece and test it experimentally since portions of the text would be destroyed.[20] Other methods have therefore traditionally been utilized in the analysis of papyrus fragments.

Thiede and his colleague first compared the Magdalen fragments with a leather scroll manuscript of the Book of Leviticus found at Cave 4 at Qumran. The Leviticus scroll is written in a style that predates the so-called later biblical uncial style, and its suggested date is the late first century. Handwriting styles, as well as the size, shape, and groupings of letters by scribes underwent a gradual process of change over the centuries, and this assists in dating a manuscript.[21] The texts of both the Magdalen fragments and the Barcelona fragments from the Gospel of Matthew use the particular type of writing that was popular in the mid-first century and share other characteristics of that period. The combination of these early fragments gives us a very reliable picture of the original Gospel of Matthew and provides a good comparison with later complete Gospel manuscripts such as the third-century Chester Beatty manuscript.[22]

The dating of the Magdalen fragments, and possibly the Barcelona fragments, by comparison to the Leviticus text at Qumran would set an initial outside date for the fragments from the Gospel of Matthew at A.D. 68 because the caves at Qumran were abandoned after that date. Thiede has stated that the similarity of the Qumran text and Magdalen fragments in overall appearance and individual letters is remarkable.[23] For example, the style of the drawings of letters on the Qumran and Magdalen fragments places them so close that they nearly touch each other, an early characteristic that

Thiede informs us was abandoned in Bible manuscripts of the second and third centuries.

A papyrus held in Paris (known as P4) from the Gospel of Luke is also believed by some papyrologists and scholars to have come from the same scribal school as the Magdalen and Barcelona fragments, though probably not from the same codex. The expert assessment based upon the similarities implies that this fragment from the Gospel of Luke should be dated not much later than the Magdalen fragments.[24] This is the earliest known fragment in existence from the Gospel of Luke.[25]

But Thiede did not base his analysis solely, or even primarily, on comparison to the Leviticus scroll. The Magdalen fragments (and by extension the Barcelona fragments and the fragment described above from the Gospel of Luke) strongly resemble a letter actually bearing a date that translates in our own calendar to July 24, A.D. 66. Thiede reports that the writing style of the dated letter is almost identical in general appearance, shape, and formation of individual letters to the Magdalen papyrus.[26] This letter was written by, or perhaps on behalf of, a farmer in Egypt to authorities at Oxyrhynchus, Egypt, to report the fact that he owned twelve lambs and had a desire to add seven new lambs to his inventory. The letter is signed, attested, and dated by three officials and by the farmer.

Another way to date or to identify the fragments is by the use of textual reconstruction, by which papyrologists will calculate such things as the average number of letters per line and note any variations from this measurement. Thiede has noted that each of the Magdalen fragments has twenty-four total lines, with an average of sixteen letters per line, with a maximum of eighteen and a minimum of fifteen.[27] This type of reconstruction of complete lines, known as stoichiometry, is a decisive instrument for the reconstruction of a text.[28] The ends and beginnings of fragmentary lines are matched against a comparative yardstick, which for the New Testament is a standard edition of a Greek text. Similarly, analysts scrutinize the spacing of words, similarities in spellings, and such stylistic elements as the projection of letters into the margin to indicate the date of the writing, or the beginning of a new paragraph or to facilitate the reconstruction of words.

The precision of the various analytical techniques is illustrated by Thiede's description of an examination of a small spot on one of the Magdalen fragments under a new microscope: an epifluorescent confocal laser scanning microscope developed and patented by Thiede and a colleague, George Masuch.[29] The question at issue was whether the spot was merely an accidental ink blot on the page or whether it was part of a letter, which would have changed the entire meaning of the sentence being reconstructed. The microscope could differentiate between twenty separate layers of the papyrus manuscript, as well as measure the height and the depth of the ink. The results were shown on a video printout that could detect even the imprint (without ink) of the scribe's pen or stylus on the papyrus. This information was then shown on a three-dimensional photograph, which supported the particular reconstruction that Thiede was proposing. The reading of the text that resulted from this examination was shown to be consistent with the original interpretation given it by Thiede. In turn, comparison of this fragment text further verified the accuracy of the third-century Chester Beatty manuscript, the oldest copy of all four Gospels.

Thiede and many other papyrologists have concluded that a small fragment found in Qumran cave 7, referred to as 7Q5, comes from a scroll containing the Gospel of Mark.[30] Since the caves were abandoned in A.D. 68, this would provide an outside date for that fragment. Because the fragment is from a scroll and not a codex, it probably dates from a much earlier time, scrolls having been used prior to the introduction of the codex.

Many biblical scholars disputed the conclusion that fragment 7Q5 is from the Gospel of Mark because they were convinced that there was no way for the Gospel to have reached the Qumran caves at such an early time, but recent studies of the Roman transportation system have undermined this argument. The caves at Qumran contained not only writings of the sect of the Essenes and other early inhabitants but also scrolls that appear to have been transported from Jerusalem, Damascus, and Rome, pointing to an efficient postal system in the Roman Empire that permitted early and easy movement of the Gospel manuscripts from one city to another.

In support of this conclusion, Thiede has noted that a jar was found in Cave 7 at Qumran that had the word *ROMA* inscribed upon it in two places, indicating its origin as Rome. Six Greek documents were also found in Cave 4, and 19 in Cave 7 at Qumran, for a total of twenty-five.[31] The normal time for postal service from Corinth, Greece, to Puteoli, Italy, has been estimated at about five days; from Rome to Alexandria, three days; from Thessaloniki, in northeastern Greece, to Ascalon, Palestine, about twelve days.[32] This easily explains the early exchange of manuscripts of the Gospels throughout various parts of the Roman Empire, including the arrival at Qumran of this fragment from the Gospel of Mark.

The controversy between biblical scholars and scientists over the fragment 7Q5 resulted in heightened scrutiny and extensive analysis by leading papyrologists, who have now concluded—based upon exhaustive study of the reconstruction of the text, the combination of letters, the application of stoichiometry, comparison to other texts from the Gospels, the study of variants in the text, and archaeological support for the analysis—that the fragment is in fact from the Gospel of Mark.[33] The methodology employed combined expert forensic examination with good detective work.

For example, the number of letters that were visible on the fragment indicated that certain words that were commonly expected to have been included on those particular lines of the Gospel were missing. These were the Greek words *epi ten gen,* meaning "on to the land." In later manuscripts of the Gospel of Mark these words appear before the words "of Gennesaret" in this passage so that the passage read "on to the land . . . of Gennesaret." The puzzle of the missing words was resolved when it was realized that they were actually added by scribes for clarity in the second, third, and fourth centuries after destruction of the town of Gennesaret by the Romans in A.D. 70. Prior to that event these missing words would have been completely unnecessary because everyone in the vicinity was familiar with the existence of the town. After its destruction the name was merely a reference to the region (see Mark 6:53).[34] This reconstruction of the text lends further support to the early date of the fragment.

As a result of all of these investigations, Thiede and most papyrologists believe that the scroll fragment is much older than A.D. 68, and that it is from the Gospel of Mark. This conclusion has been summarized by Orsolina Montevecchi, honorary president of the International Papyrologists' Association: "I do not think that there can be any doubt about the identification of 7Q5."[35]

The redating of the Magdalen fragments and the associated fragments from the Gospel of Luke, as well as the Qumran fragment from the Gospel of Mark, crystallizes the early dating for those three Gospels. It permits us to assume that the writers were alive at a date early enough to reasonably infer that they had the opportunity to observe the events reported, as required under the rules of evidence. Hard extrinsic evidence such as this for a particular date requires those who would argue against it to provide equivalent extrinsic proof outside of reasoned analysis.

The Gospel of John is believed to have been the last one written. The earliest known papyrus fragment of the Gospel of John, known as the St. John Papyrus P–52 (or, John Rylands Greek 457), is currently dated to the first quarter of the second century, though Thiede believes that the actual date is probably much earlier. The fragment is held by the John Rylands University Library in Manchester, England.[36]

Again, this Gospel clearly reflects social and political conditions in Palestine, particularly Jerusalem, of the mid-first century. Just as important, it does *not* reflect the situation that existed between Christians vis à vis Jews, or of either group vis à vis Rome, after A.D. 70. It presents Jesus in a particularly early and mid-century Jewish way as the hope and light of the world but transcending the legal limitations of Judaism.[37]

The Gospel of John also contains many contemporary and familiar topographical references to places and things that were not in existence after A.D. 70. Two clear indications that at the time it was written Jerusalem was still in existence can be illustrated, and many scholars have accepted these passages as absolute truth of the early date of the Gospel.

First, in the Gospel of John, Jesus is described as healing a man who had been paralyzed for thirty-eight years, at the sheep pool in a building in Jerusalem that has also now been historically identified by archaeologists (John 5:2). The author of the Gospel uses the *present tense* to describe the sheep pool: "Now there *is* in Jerusalem by the sheep gate a pool, which *is* called in Hebrew Bethesda, having five porticoes" (John 5:2, emphasis added).The natural and reasonable inference is that the author of this Gospel was writing when the building was still standing. By A.D. 70 the Romans had completely destroyed the building and its porticoes. The building at that location that has recently been found dates to the fifth century; however, excavations have revealed two huge, deep rock-cut cisterns nearby, with stairs that originally led to the bottom of the pools, and these have been dated by the surviving masonry as being of the time of Jesus.[38] This same building is believed to be mentioned in the Copper Scroll of the Dead Sea Scrolls as Beth Eshdathayin, the "House of the Twin Pools."[39]

Second, in another passage the author of the Gospel of John quoted the Jews standing nearby as stating that "it took forty-six years to build *this* temple" (emphasis added). The reference by the author is to the temple that was physically near the group as they spoke to Jesus. Construction began during the reign of Herod the Great in approximately 20 to 19 B.C., and although the temple proper was completed in approximately A.D. 18, construction of the entire temple complex continued until about A.D. 60. Chronologically, this statement can be calculated to have been made at about A.D. 28 to 30, during the last years of the ministry of Jesus as reported by the Gospels.[40]

Irenaeus, bishop of Gaul in about A.D. 180, was a student of Polycarp, a disciple of John, and associated with others who had contact with first-generation Christians.[41] He wrote that John lived until the reign of the emperor Trajan, which began in A.D. 98.[42] Robinson, however, in a carefully reasoned study has pointed out that there is no positive reason to suppose that the Gospel was written near the end of John's life. In an extensive analysis giving consideration to the historical points of reference established in this Gospel, Robinson has dated it reliably at A.D. 65, with the possibility of an earlier draft having been prepared between A.D. 50 and 55.[43]

The new redating of the Gospel of Matthew, the comparative associated redating of the Gospels of Mark and Luke, and the dating for the Gospel of John require the Gospels now to be analyzed completely differently from texts believed to have been written years later. The early dating of the manuscripts clearly permits a belief that the authors of the Gospels were potential eyewitnesses, alive at the time of the events, with an opportunity to observe personally those events. Moreover, the early dating undermines the assertion of critics that, since memory can be altered by the passage of time, the Gospels are not reliable as evidence, or that they were merely stories derived from myths or legends.

In addition, the firsthand nature of the Gospel testimony is often suggested by affirmative statements by the authors in the narratives that the events were observed by the authors as eyewitnesses, which is also corroborated by statements in other

New Testament writings. This point was particularly emphasized in the Gospels, and authentication of the eyewitness nature of the observations is abundant (see 2 Pet. 1:16; 1 John 1:1–3; Luke 1:1–3; Acts 1:1–3; 1 Cor. 15:6–8; John 20:30, 31; 21:24; Acts 10:39–42; 1 Pet. 5:1; Acts 1:9).[44] For example, in the Gospel of John, the author emphasized that the account of the soldier's piercing of Jesus' side on the cross was based upon the author's own eyewitness observation. Other New Testament writings also contain numerous reports of eyewitnesses to the actual resurrection of Jesus (Luke 24:48; Acts 1:8; Acts 2:32; 3:15; 4:33; 5:32; 10:39, 41; 13:31; 22:15; 23:11; 1 Cor. 15:4–19; 1 John 1:2).

The early dating of these Gospels suggests that they were actually in circulation at a time when the people who participated in the reported events were still alive. The people who would have received these Gospels in all likelihood were the same ones who were present when some of these events occurred and additionally were familiar with the oral history of those events. These people would have acted as a natural safeguard against inaccuracy in the testimony, and they would not have adopted teachings that they believed to be false. The importance of these events to the people actually involved in them is evident to us today, not only through the sacrifices that many of them were willing to bear in support of these principles but also by the swift establishment of the Christian church throughout the entire region.

Critics who believe that the Gospels were not written by people living at the time of the events reported no longer have a basis for that position; the Gospels appear to have been written almost contemporaneously (from a historical perspective) with the last events that occurred, the crucifixion and resurrection of Jesus.

It is interesting to contrast the uniform acceptance of the validity and authorship of other historical documents with the way the Gospels are generally viewed by scholars. The closest time interval between any ancient writing and its original form, other than the New Testament, is probably the *three-century interval* between the original writings of Virgil and the date of the first known existing manuscript. In contrast, at the most only thirty or so years occurred between the events reported in the Gospels and the date assigned to the first fragments that match later manuscripts word for word. The primary historical works of Tacitus, who wrote at the end of the first century, are preserved in only two manuscripts, one dated in the ninth century and one in the eleventh.[45] The *Iliad*, by Homer, is preserved in 643 manuscripts; the works of Euripides, in 330 manuscripts; and the *History of Rome*, by Velleius Paterculus, was preserved in only one incomplete manuscript, lost in the seventeenth century; whereas there are over twenty-five thousand early handwritten copies of the Bible in Greek, Latin, and other languages.[46] It is submitted therefore that the historical reliability of the Gospels should be tested against the same criteria as other works. In that regard, Greenleaf has pointed out that the entire text of the Roman Civil Law, *Corpus Juris Civilis*, has been received as established authority based upon much weaker evidence of its authority.[47]

Historical circumstances, the four Gospels' first-person style of reporting in the context of early and mid-first-century society, and the early dating of the papyrus fragments of the manuscripts all provide us with evidence that the authors were alive at the time the events occurred and that they had the *opportunity* to have been present at the events to which they testify, thus meeting the standards required to show firsthand knowledge under the Federal Rules of Evidence.

The attribution of the authorship of the Gospels to actual individuals is supported by substantially contemporaneous historical writings contained in the New Testament, and by writings outside the New Testament. These assertions are based upon the oral history and understanding in the community from the time of the death of Jesus through the dates of such writings. For example, scholars almost all agree that a letter from Paul to the Christian community in Corinth dated A.D. 54 to 56 preserves very early oral teachings about the resurrection of Jesus. These words, in the form of an early creed, are written in a style that predates the author, using primitive Aramaic language that is different from the rest of the letter (see 1 Cor. 15:4–7).[48]

A writing referred to as the *Didache* (or *The Teaching of the Twelve Apostles*) appears to contain an early reference to a written "Gospel" of Jesus, in a specific rather than a general sense, which is to be received from each apostle as if it came from Jesus himself.[49] The actual dating of the *Didache* is uncertain, but the judgment of many scholars is that it reflects a very early period, perhaps even predating the actual writing of any of the four Gospels. Additionally, in A.D. 95, Clement of Rome appears to have used material from what are now known as the Gospels of Matthew and Luke in a letter written to Christians in the city of Corinth.[50] The letter also stated that "the Apostles received the Gospel for us from the Lord Jesus Christ . . . they went forth with the glad tidings that the kingdom of God should come."[51] A recently discovered work indicates that by

A.D. 140 a compilation of the Gospels, Acts, the letters of Paul, Hebrews, and the Book of Revelation was already in existence, and that the writings were generally accepted as authoritative.[52]

A determination by the jury that the authors of the Gospels were writers with firsthand knowledge of the events reported is not dependent upon establishing the actual individual relationships. But knowing who the writers actually were will add depth and richness to the understanding of the nature of this testimony. The individualization of the testimony further corroborates the firsthand nature of the testimony. Let us therefore examine the written attributions of authorship of the four Gospels being offered into evidence.

Based upon the prior analysis, including the recent redating of the Magdalen fragments from the Gospel attributed to Matthew, we may reasonably believe that the Gospel of Matthew was written within approximately thirty-three to thirty-six years of the death of Jesus, no later than the comparative Egyptian letter dated A.D. 66 from a farmer described above, and probably much earlier. The earliest historical account of the attribution of the writing to the apostle Matthew comes from Papias, bishop of Hierapolis in Asia Minor, writing about A.D. 130. As preserved in the writings of Eusebius, bishop of Caesarea and a church historian who lived between A.D. 270 and 340, Papias wrote the following in an apparent reference to the Gospel of Matthew:

> Matthew compiled the Logia in the Hebrew
> [Aramaic] speech, and everyone translated them as
> best he could.[53]

Additionally, a document known as the Anti-Marcionite Prologue, written near the end of the second century, refers to

Matthew's writing in Judea. The historian Eusebius also referred to this Gospel as having been written before the departure of Matthew from Palestine.[54] Irenaeus wrote:

> Matthew published his gospel among the Hebrews in their own tongue, when Peter and Paul were preaching the Gospel in Rome and founding the church there.[55]

The Gospel of Matthew is offered to you, the jury, as written testimonial evidence given by the apostle Matthew, also known as Levi, one of the original twelve apostles referred to in the Gospels, an eyewitness to the events reported. He was Jewish and held the post of a tax gatherer under Roman authority, apparently with responsibility for collecting taxes, duties, and customs in the region. His presence at the events and during the time reported in his Gospel is also mentioned in other books of the New Testament.

Because the Magdalen fragments, dated by Thiede no later than A.D. 66, are written in Greek, and Papias states that the original Gospel was written in Aramaic, we may also infer that an original manuscript was written by Matthew at a date even earlier than that of the Greek Magdalen fragments. Some scholars have argued that the original Gospel of Matthew was written in Greek; however, that speculation, which is based solely upon scholarly interpretation and no empirical evidence, requires a supposition that Papias, who wrote in the early part of the second century, was either wrong or confused.[56] In contrast, Ignatius, a contemporary of Papias who wrote about A.D. 115, described him as being "a man well skilled in all manner of learning, and well acquainted with the Scriptures."[57] Papias was also careful to authenticate his own extensive investigations of the origins of the Gospels derived from both writings and oral teachings. In work preserved by Eusebius, Papias stated that whenever he was in the presence of the "elders" or someone who had been a companion of the apostles, or any of the other disciples of Jesus, he would inquire about their "sayings" to obtain personal authentication of those reports.

> But I will not be unwilling to put down . . . whatsoever instruction I received with care from the elders and stored up with care in my memory, assuring you at the same time of their truth. For I did not, like the multitude, take pleasure in those who spoke much, but in those who taught the truth; nor in those who related strange commandments, but in those who rehearsed the commandments given by the Lord to faith, and proceeding from truth itself.[58]

Papias was further described by Irenaeus as "a hearer" of the apostle John, and a companion of Polycarp, "a man of primitive times."[59] Another early fragment refers to Papias as a disciple of John, and the Anti-Marcionite Prologue also refers to Papias as "John's dear disciple."[60]

Although the books written by Papias are now lost with the exception of a few fragments, other ancient writers have preserved relevant quotations from his early writings. There is no reason to suppose, therefore, that Papias was either confused or wrong in his conclusions.

Further support for an earlier Aramaic original manuscript by the apostle Matthew appears in Irenaeus's statement in the second century, noted above, that Matthew wrote a Gospel for the Hebrews in their own dialect. Additionally, as late as the fourth century, Jerome wrote that the Hebrew Gospel of

Matthew was preserved at that time in the library at Caesarea.[61] Raymond Brown in his recent study on the New Testament reported that Clement of Alexandria and Origen, early church historians from the second century and the early part of the third century, also accepted that the Greek manuscript of the Gospel of Matthew was translated from Aramaic.[62]

In the opinion of many scholars, Matthew's clear preservation of Aramaic idioms in his use of Greek strongly supports the Aramaic origin of that Gospel.[63] The structure and style of the writing also indicate the Aramaic nature of the writing. For example, the lineage of Jesus is traced as it would have been by a Jewish writer for Jewish readers. If the Aramaic manuscript was written first, the date of the original of the Gospel of Matthew must be somewhat earlier than A.D. 66, the date assigned to the Greek Magdalen fragments.

A man named John Mark is traditionally identified as the author of the Gospel of Mark. Again, the earliest historical source of authorship is a statement found in the writings of Papias, as preserved by Eusebius:

> Mark, having become the interpreter of Peter, wrote down accurately whatsoever he [Peter] remembered. It was not, however, in exact order that he related the sayings or deeds of Christ, for he neither heard the Lord nor accompanied him. But afterwards, as I said, he accompanied Peter, who accommodated his instructions to the necessities [of his hearers], but with no intention of giving a regular narrative of the Lord's sayings. Wherefore Mark made no mistake in thus writing some things as he [Peter] remembered them. For one thing he took especial care, not to

omit anything that he had heard and not to put anything fictious into the statements.[64]

Irenaeus wrote that "Mark, the disciple and interpreter of
Peter, himself handed down to us in writing the substance of
Peter's preaching."[65] Clement of Alexandria wrote that Peter
was alive at the time that this Gospel was written. Eusebius
recorded that Peter "was pleased" and "authorized the book to
be read in the churches."[66] An additional writing of Clement of
Alexandria that has been preserved only in Latin, states the following:

> Mark, the follower of Peter, while Peter publicly
> preached the gospel at Rome before some of Caesar's
> equites [knights], adduced many testimonies to
> Christ, in order that thereby they might be able to
> commit to memory what was . . . spoken by Peter . . .
> [and he] . . . wrote entirely what is called the Gospel
> according to Mark.[67]

Papias, and later Irenaeus, and the Anti-Marcionite
Prologue all used the word *interpreter* when referring to the
work of Mark and his relationship to the apostle Peter. Papias
further specifically emphasized that in this role Mark was
extremely accurate, and careful neither to omit information nor
to include any false statement.

F. F. Bruce, in a study of the origins of the Gospels, has
noted that this belief that Mark wrote his Gospel as an agent
for Peter is also supported by testimony of scholars in recent
years based on the internal structure and form of this Gospel,
which is similar to certain portions of the New Testament Book
of Acts that contain teachings identified specifically with Peter.[68]

Additionally, the Greek text of the Gospel of Mark

appears to preserve an "Aramaic Galilaean" idiom such as Peter would have used.[69] And, C. H. Turner's linguistic studies published in 1924 and 1925 note that Mark often uses the first-person pronouns "we" and "our" to describe events that occurred during the life of Jesus and Peter and specifically refer to Peter.[70] Other scholars believe that the Gospel of Mark contains some references to events in which Mark actually participated, though that is not entirely free from doubt (see, for example, Mark 14:51, 52).[71]

It is thought that Mark was converted to Christianity by Peter, one of the original twelve apostles of Jesus. The Latin phrases contained in the Gospel indicate that Mark wrote this book for the use of Gentile converts,[72] an idea corroborated by contemporaneous and nearly contemporaneous writers as well as by the historical context and references in this Gospel.

Mark is believed to have initially been a "helper" for a missionary team organized by Paul and Barnabas in approximately A.D. 46, as well as having had a close relationship with Peter, who described Mark as his spiritual "son" in a letter to Jewish Christians in approximately A.D. 62 to 64 (see 1 Pet. 5:13).[73] Mark may literally have been an interpreter for Peter, since it is presumed that Peter spoke primarily Aramaic whereas evidence indicates that Mark's primary language would have been Greek. Federal courts hold that so long as the interpreter has sufficient capacity and no motive to misrepresent the information transmitted, the interpreter is treated as the agent of the person making the original statement, no more than a conduit for the thoughts and words of the principal.[74]

The term *interpreter* could also refer, however, to the use of Mark as a *hyperetai,* or helper or agent through whom Peter was speaking. Such helpers were not unusual in those times, and they were often utilized for the recording of events throughout the period reported in the New Testament. This involved the use of secretaries, or trusted helpers, to write such documents as the Gospels, Acts, and letters of Paul, who was a Jew and a Roman citizen who lived in Palestine during the time of Jesus and who was converted after the crucifixion (Acts 13:5; 1 Pet. 5:12; Rom. 16:22). The role of the helper was an important one; helpers were more than scribes, but they were not the authors of the scripts. Biblical scholars have noted the difference between the books of Peter, the first being written in educated Greek, indicating the use of a helper, and the second being written in a more Hebraic style. Peter refers to this helper as "Silvanus," a "trustworthy brother" in a letter contained in the New Testament (1 Pet. 5:12). The authority of the persons whose thoughts or teachings were to be conveyed through the use of these helpers was never in doubt. For example, Paul occasionally verified his authorship in letters despite the use of a helper by adding his personal signature: "The greeting is in my own hand—Paul"(1 Cor. 16:21).

Authorship of the Gospel of Luke is attributed by various other writings of the New Testament to a person who was a companion of Paul. Irenaeus wrote that "Luke, the follower of Paul, set down in a book the gospel preached by his teacher."[75] A prologue to the New Testament written in the second century also refers to Luke as being from Antioch, and adds that he died in Greece.[76] The Muratorian Canon, dating from about A.D. 170, stated that the Gospel of Luke was composed "in his own name on the basis of report."[77]

The style of writing in this Gospel is more scholarly than the others, and the focus on medical aspects has led many to believe that Luke was a physician. That belief is supported by a statement in a letter from Paul to the church at Colosse, written in approximately A.D. 60, referring to Luke as a physician (Col. 4:14).

This Gospel appears to have been written in the nature of an investigative report, at the request of or for the benefit of a particular person (it is addressed to Theophilus), as well as for the benefit of Gentile converts. The Gospel begins with these words:

> Inasmuch as many have undertaken to compile an account of the things accomplished among us, just as those who from the beginning were eyewitnesses and servants of the word have handed them down to us, it seemed fitting for me as well, having investigated everything carefully from the beginning, to write it out for you in consecutive order, most excellent Theophilus; so that you might know the exact truth about the things you have been taught (Luke 1:1–4).

Scholars do not know who Theophilus was. Although some firsthand knowledge is implied, Luke does not take the position in this passage that he was an actual eyewitness to every event. He uses the pronoun "we," suggesting that he was a firsthand witness to some of the things that he reports.

In his Gospel, Luke was very precise. He carefully placed the time of certain events in historical context, for example, by reference to the reign of certain Roman emperors or governors of various regions. The Gospel of Luke appears to have been written after extremely diligent research, an intent indicated by his introduction.

Luke also wrote the Book of Acts in the New Testament, which continues the story begun in this Gospel, commencing after the death and resurrection of Jesus. The Book of Acts and other writings of the New Testament give evidence that Luke spent many years in the company of Paul in and near Jerusalem, Caesarea, and Rome and that he knew some of the apostles, members of the family of Jesus, and members of the Herod family.[78]

The first six chapters of the Gospel of Luke are contained in a papyrus held in Paris, known as P–4. As discussed above, Thiede has dated this document close to the date of the Magdalen fragments, but slightly later because, though it appears to have been prepared by a scribe in the same school, it has not been established that it came from the same codex as that of the Magdalen fragments.[79] Thiede believes that this is the earliest existing manuscript of the Gospel of Luke.

The Gospel of John expressly states that it was written by the apostle John, who was an eyewitness to the events recorded, though occasional references to John in the third person also indicate that the Gospel was written with the assistance of helpers. The Gospel ends with the authentication of the author, or of the helper on his behalf, as follows:

This is the disciple who bears witness of these things, and wrote these things; and we know that his witness is true (John 21:24).

The third-person reference is to a disciple described throughout the Gospel of John as "the disciple whom Jesus loved." By analysis of the internal evidence of the testimony, that is, the structure of the narrative, most scholars have accepted that the reference is to the apostle John. The reference to "we" in the quoted passage is believed to be to a group of friends and disciples who acted as helpers, or scribes, and edited and assured public distribution of the Gospel on his behalf.[80] This is the only one of the four Gospels that affirmatively contains a statement claiming to be written by a direct observation of an eyewitness. For example, the apostle is mentioned as being present at the Last Supper prior to the crucifixion of Jesus, being with Jesus in the Garden of Gethsemane after the last supper, as an eyewitness at the foot of the cross and with Peter at the tomb of Jesus after his burial, and at a resurrection appearance of Jesus in Galilee.[81]

John's authorship of this Gospel is referred to by many of the early Christian writers. Polycarp, who had been a disciple of John and was burned alive for his beliefs, and Ignatius, who died in the arena in Rome in A.D. 115, were both greatly influenced by this particular Gospel. Ignatius referred to John as one of the twelve disciples of Jesus and quoted from the Gospel.[82] The Gnostic Basilides, written in approximately A.D. 130, and Justin Martyr, writing at about A.D. 150, both referred to the apostle John. Tatian, a disciple of Justin Martyr, writing in approximately the same period, mentions the Gospel itself. Other works from the second century by Clement of Alexandria, Tertullian of Carthage, and the Gnostic Heracleon all support the view that John was the author of this Gospel.[83] Irenaeus wrote about A.D. 180 that John himself produced his Gospel.[84] A passage in a prologue written for the Gospel of John near the end of the second century also states that John wrote it himself and that the book was dictated to a helper for publication.[85] The prologue derived this information from Papias's *Exposition of the Oracles of the Lord,* written in approximately A.D. 130 and since lost.

The style of the Gospel of John indicates that it was written from the perspective of a Jew but with a view to those who must be brought into the Christian fold. He writes with obvious familiarity of Jewish customs and the portions of the Old Testament that were prescribed for reading by Jews in the synagogue and at religious festivals. He also shows a familiarity with Jewish laws of evidence, the habits of the rabbis and high priests, and methods of argument that has generally impressed scholars.[86]

The Gospel of John speaks to your soul. It is the most beautifully written of the four and contains not only a report of events observed but also the testimony of the witness about his understanding, or opinion, as to what these events actually meant. Scholars have criticized John's Gospel because of this style, which they have characterized as indicating a much later period of writing, and because of the interpretation which John provides. This style of imagery and writing was at one time grounds for the belief that the fourth Gospel was created by someone beyond the scope of the generation living at the time that Jesus lived, around A.D. 100 or later.

That thinking has been eroded, however, not only by other evidence supporting the earlier dating of the Gospel, described above, but also by the discovery of the Dead Sea Scrolls. Although the Dead Sea Scrolls do not appear to contain any direct reference to Jesus or the apostles, the writings of the sect of Essenes and others inhabiting the cave dwellings employ the same type of language and imagery as that used in the Gospel of John. The Dead Sea Scrolls have established an early date for the use of such imagery, because the latest possible date for the manuscripts found in the caves of Qumran was A.D. 68.[87] They show that the Gospel of John reflects the very heart and soul of Palestine before the Roman invasion.

A comparison of the use of similar phraseology in the Gospel of John and the Dead Sea Scrolls is revealing. Such phrases as "conflict between light and darkness," the "spirit of truth," the "light of life," "walking in the darkness," "children of light," and "eternal life" in the Dead Sea Scrolls give evidence that John's style of writing was typical of the early and mid-first century, in contrast to previous assertions of scholars.[88] Comparison to the Dead Sea Scrolls, which are dated no later than A.D. 68, further confirms a date for the Gospel of John prior to the destruction of Jerusalem and the temple by the Romans.

Additionally, F. F. Bruce has noticed what he calls a "remarkable" similarity between the style and imagery of the Gospel of John and an early collection of Christian hymns from the period between A.D. 50 and 100. Likewise, Robinson has compared the similarities between this imagery and the speculative and mystical influence of the Old Testament that is evident in other New Testament writings that have been dated between A.D. 50 and 60.[89]

The inclusion of personal thoughts and interpretation constituting opinion in the testimony of the apostle John does not diminish its value as evidence in a court of law under the Federal Rules of Evidence:

> *If the witness is not testifying as an expert, the witness' testimony in the form of opinions or inferences is limited to those opinions or inferences which are (a) rationally based on the perception of the witness and (b) helpful to a clear understanding of the witness' testimony or the determination of a fact in issue.*[90]

John's testimony in the form of opinions or inferences is admissible, so long as it is rationally linked to what he actually observed and is helpful to a further understanding of the issues to be resolved. His opinions often deal with cause and effect in connection with the Gospel events. Like the illuminated manuscripts of old, the written thoughts of John add color and perspective to the black and white sketches presented by Matthew, Mark, and Luke.

In summary therefore, the legal nature of the authorship of the Gospels is presented as follows:

First, the Gospels of Matthew and John appear to have been written by eyewitnesses to the events.

Second, the Gospel of Mark was written by or on behalf of or as an agent for Peter, an eyewitness. Federal Rule of Evidence 602 allows a witness to testify, even though that witness may not have knowledge in the *literal* sense.[91] Statements made by Mark without evidence of any motive for misrepresentation, to the extent they are determined to be made as an interpreter or helper for Peter, will be treated as statements of Peter and would be permitted as evidence based upon firsthand knowledge in a court of law.[92] As discussed above, through analysis of the internal structure and form of the narrative, expert scholars over the years have supported the notion that Peter is the source of this Gospel.[93]

The relationship of Peter and Mark, as evidenced by other Christian and non-Christian historical writings, further corroborates the belief that Mark wrote his Gospel on behalf of Peter, as his agent. Under the common law, statements of a person acting as an agent for a principal, as determined by all aspects of the relationship, will be treated as the statements of the principal.[94] Courts have commonly upheld this idea and have determined that it is immaterial whether or not the declarant was expressly authorized to speak on behalf of his principal. It is sufficient that the statement accompanies conduct authorized by the principal.[95] Consistent with this legal principle and the evidence of experts who have examined the internal structure and form of this Gospel, as presented above, the majority opinion of historians and biblical scholars for two thousand years has been that the Gospel of Mark was written by Mark at the direction or dictation of Peter. This Gospel then stands primarily as the testimony of an eyewitness, the apostle Peter.

Third, it is fairly clear that at least large portions of the Gospel of Luke were written by someone other than an eyewitness. We have already established that as evidence these Gospels are all admissible for the jury's consideration as ancient writings. Greenleaf has also noted, however, that if these Gospels were inquiries, gravely undertaken and pursued, by a person of competent intelligence, sagacity, and integrity, and they were undertaken at the request of a person in authority or by a desire to serve the public, then the results would be legally admissible evidence in a court of law, even if the report was voluntarily undertaken.[96] Because of the careful, extremely detailed examination of the events reported, even if the Gospel of Luke were held out merely as the investigative work of a contemporary historian, it would be entitled to belief.[97]

Additionally, statements made by a person regarding personal history, even when the person who is the subject of the testimony is not a relative of the witness, will be admissible and will not be excluded by the hearsay rule so long as the witness was intimately associated with the subject of the report and would be likely to have accurate information concerning the matters involved.[98] The Gospel of Luke also fulfills these latter criteria.

The Gospel of Luke, therefore, while not clearly eyewitness testimony, stands as a valid historical report or investigation, gravely undertaken by a witness who was intimately associated with the subject of the report. Because this Gospel corroborates the facts set forth in the other three Gospels, we are entitled to take it into consideration in our analysis and to review its overall credibility, including the competence and integrity of the reporter.

It is within the jury's discretion to decide whether all of this evidence shows that the testimony of the Gospels of Mark and Luke constitute eyewitness reports. Most important, under the theory that the Gospel of Mark was written by Mark as an interpreter or helper for the apostle Peter, this Gospel may quite reasonably be determined by the jury to be in fact a third eyewitness account, that of the apostle Peter. Regardless, to the extent these two Gospels support the testimony of the apostles John and Matthew, they become corroborative links in the chain of evidence. Even if you, the jury, determine that either of these two Gospels does not represent eyewitness testimony, they corroborate the testimony of those who were eyewitnesses with whom they were intimately related, and they record matters of public record and significant public interest.

To keep things in perspective, remember that one eyewitness is sufficient under the law, with convincing corroborating evidence, to support a murder conviction in the United States; the testimony of two eyewitnesses is very difficult to overcome.

Finally, the Gospels do contain stories, such as the birth of Jesus, that were not observed by the authors. The jury has the option of considering only those portions of the Gospels that it believes to be based upon firsthand knowledge.[99] When a witness testifies partly to things that he or she has actually seen or heard, and partly from what was told by another, a practical compromise under the rules governing evidence is to admit the information based on firsthand knowledge and exclude the remaining testimony. Regarding the issues in our case, however, Matthew, John, and Peter (speaking through Mark) all purport to have actually observed the resurrection of Jesus.

In summary, evidence establishes that the Gospels were written by people who were actually alive at the time that Jesus lived, died, and came back to life, not by unknown writers many generations later. In this case, sufficient evidence has been offered to present to the jury the Gospels of John, Matthew, and Mark as testimony based upon personal knowledge of the events at issue in our case as described in those Gospels. The Gospel of Luke is presented to the jury as being an investigative report of events of public and historical importance, carefully prepared by a reporter at a time contemporaneous, or nearly contemporaneous, with the events that occurred. It is presented as a link in the chain of evidence that corroborates the testimony of the other three.

CHAPTER FOUR

Cross-Examination on Originality

We would be remiss if we did not subject our witnesses to critical cross-examination. A cross-examination of these witnesses will reveal that the Gospels of Matthew, Mark, and Luke have some material in common. For that reason they are sometimes referred to as the "synoptic" Gospels, and this has given rise to the so-called "synoptic problem." This is essentially a challenge to the belief that these three Gospels are all original testimony of the authors. In other words, a claim has been made that one or two of the Gospel writers copied from the third. The Gospel of John is not included in this analysis because it is very different from the three synoptic Gospels.

Some scholars who deny that these Gospels present *original* testimony of three different witnesses have taken the position that the Gospel of Mark was used as a basic outline by Matthew and Luke. The Gospel of Matthew, however, is much more extensive than that of either Mark or Luke. Regardless, it is admitted by these critics that there are many unique individual passages in each of Matthew, Mark, and Luke that do not appear in the others. There are also many discrepancies or inconsistencies even among the common passages in all three of these Gospels. For passages in common between Matthew and Luke that are not found in Mark, these critics further assert that a common source document exists, which they have labeled Q, for Quelle (German for "source").

The theory that the Gospels of Matthew and Luke were copied from Mark is somewhat weakened by the argument of some scholars who believe that the first Gospel was composed by Matthew in Aramaic and that the Gospel of Matthew was used as a norm by Mark and Luke.[1] The latter hypothesis—if a basic outline narrative was indeed provided, it would have been provided by Matthew—is supported by the statement of Papias that Matthew first compiled the "Logia" in Aramaic and that everyone thereafter translated it.[2] Aramaic was probably the language most commonly used by Jesus and his apostles (although romanization of the area also resulted in the familiarity of most people with Greek). Clement of Alexandria, Origen, and Eusebius also appeared to believe that Matthew's Gospel came first.[3] The question of whether the Gospel of Mark or Matthew came first remains an open issue, however, and the answer is not critical to our case. It is the *originality* of the testimony that the jury must now consider, not the priority of authorship.

The theories that Mark was copied by Matthew and Luke, or that Matthew was copied by Mark and Luke, or that a Q source was used, are controversial. After many decades of investigation, no Q source nor any ancient reference to such a source has been found.[4] Scholars who believe that the Q source was used by Matthew, Mark, or Luke in the original creation of those Gospels hold that Q contains no narrative, only a collection of quotations or sayings of Jesus. This hypothesis holds that the Q source existed before the Gospels and that the narratives were merely stories created generations later to surround these few quotations in an attempt to establish church doctrine.

Undermining this hypothesis is the early dating of the papyrus fragments that contain not only quotations from Jesus but also extensive narrative and quotations of other people. As we have seen, these fragments have been matched word for word with the later complete manuscripts of the various Gospels, and the text is identical. The entire Gospels, narrative and all, have therefore been shown to have been in existence at such an early date that there is no reason, without evidence, to assume that a Q document was the source. Because of the new early dating assigned to the three synoptic Gospels, the Q source, if such a document existed, would have to have been written almost immediately upon the death of Jesus.

As to the assertion that the Gospels were copied one from the other, a more straightforward response to this challenge is that the similarity among the three Gospels arose out of the fact that they were all derived from, or based upon, the same oral teachings by Jesus.[5] The accurate transmission of religious teachings was considered to be a sacred task by the Jews and early Christians. Memorization of oral teachings was traditional among Jews and had been for literally hundreds of years. In fact, some rabbis memorized the entire Old Testament. Scholars have also noted that many of the quotations of Jesus have a poetical structure, making them more susceptible to memorization. In that regard, it is interesting to note that many of the passages that are so similar as to require some explanation also include the slight discrepancies that would be expected of the texts reported from trained—but not perfectly accurate—memory.

Scribes were also trained in shorthand writing; this was a required skill.[6] For example, a text written on leather and entirely in Greek shorthand has been found near the Dead Sea.[7] It dates from the early second century at the latest. Although difficult to decipher, it appears to be a Christian text because a monogram associated with reference to Christ is included. Shorthand was apparently used as an everyday tool by both Jewish and Gentile writers of the period. Many scholars believe that Matthew as a customs or tax official in Galilee would have had knowledge of this method, permitting him to preserve many of the teachings of Jesus verbatim.[8]

Another explanation for the similarity in the three Gospels comes from scholars who have noted that the custom in the time of Jesus was to stereotype the forms in which religious teachings were presented. A modern comparison to this method of communication can be illustrated by the stereotypical manner in which a police report is given in court. The report is usually unadorned, conforming closely to the course of events at issue in the case, in order to preserve accuracy.[9] Very similar narratives would be an expected result if this is a correct analysis.

Finally, the fact that the Gospels of Matthew, Mark, and Luke were written by people at approximately the same time, people who all knew each other extremely well and who may have lived together for the greater part of several years, could account for much of the similarity. The apostle Peter is a particularly strong common link to all three of these Gospels. Additionally, the events that occurred and were reported were of a startling nature, culminating in the crucifixion of someone deeply loved and his resurrection, which would have been stunning. That these events would leave a deep and significant impression upon the style and manner of reporting is not surprising.

A comparison between different New Testament translations of passages generally included within the synoptic problem makes it clear that twentieth-century styles of translation may have affected the analysis of the text by modern scholars. A study originally prepared in the 1930s, and updated in 1956 by Burton H. Throckmorton Jr. (using the 1952 Revised Standard Version of the Bible), compared the corresponding common passages of these three Gospels in parallel columns.[10] Because this study was later revised, for clarity we will refer to it as the "1956 Throckmorton study." The following text was given as an example of identical wording, suggesting that two of the manuscripts were copied from the third. In the portion of the sentence under review we find a request for the body of Jesus after his death, made by a follower of Jesus to Pilate. The follower, Joseph of Arimathea, "went to Pilate and asked for the body of Jesus."

The 1956 Throckmorton study reveals *identical* language for this passage for each of the three Gospels. Conversely, in other versions, or translations, popularly relied upon by current scholars (including a later revision of the 1956 Throckmorton study based upon a different translation), the same passages are far from identical. Here is an example taken from the King James Version from corresponding passages to those in the 1956 Throckmorton study[11]:

Matthew 27:58	Mark 15:43	Luke 23:52
He went to Pilate, and begged the body of Jesus. Then Pilate commanded the body to be delivered.	Joseph of Arimathaea, an honourable counselor, which also waited for the kingdom of God, came, and went in boldly unto Pilate, and craved the body of Jesus.	This man went unto Pilate, and begged the body of Jesus.

Clearly, if the 1956 Throckmorton study had used the King James Version, the passages set forth above would not have counted as being identical texts. Additionally, in a 1995 text that provides parallels among seven English language versions of each passage of each Gospel of the New Testament, the same passage which we have reviewed above was found to be translated differently in each one![12] It is obvious that there is room for error in a comparison of the interdependence of the text of the three Gospels as a result of the particular translation being utilized in these modern studies. This is especially a cause for some skepticism in so far as the interdependence of the Gospels is based upon a comparison of the commonality of the texts where the identical text is not fairly extensive and clear.

With respect to the portions of the three Gospels that critics have alleged to be interdependent, from my own study I have concluded that there are three possible types of similar passages included in the synoptic problem. Unfortunately, most biblical scholars who have focused on the synoptic problem have failed to make this distinction to their readers. This analysis is based upon the comparison given in the 1956 Throckmorton study which overall provided an objective and straightforward presentation of similar passages of the Gospels of Matthew, Mark, and Luke set forth in parallel columns.[13] Comparisons of these passages are extremely difficult to make because the narrative structures of the three Gospels do not necessarily follow each other chronologically.

First to be considered are those passages that are very similar in story line or concept but that are not identical in wording. An example of this would be the following passages from the Gospels of Matthew and Mark:

Matthew 13:31–32 (RSV)	Mark 4:30–32 (RSV)
Another parable he put before them, saying, "The kingdom of heaven is like a grain of mustard seed which a man took and sowed in his field; it is the smallest of all seeds, but when it has grown it is the greatest of shrubs and becomes a tree, so that the birds of the air come and make nests in its branches."	And he said, "With what can we compare the kingdom of God, or what parable shall we use for it? It is like a grain of mustard seed, which, when sown upon the ground, is the smallest of all the seeds on earth; yet when it is sown it grows up and becomes the greatest of all shrubs, and puts forth large branches, so that the birds of the air can make nests in its shade."

As you can see, though the parables are very similar, they are not so similar that coincidence must be ruled out. This is particularly true when you consider that the witnesses are both repeating their recollections of an important statement that they claim to have heard at the same time from the same person in the same place. This is not only what one would expect to hear from two witnesses testifying to the same event in a courtroom, but it is what one would hope for. This type of similarity does not diminish the originality of the testimony; rather, such immaterial differences strengthen the testimony, indicating they were not copied but were individual recollections.

The second type of comparison generally included in analyses of the synoptic problem is of passages that contain parts of sentences with identical structure or words, with the remainder of the sentence and sometimes the context of the statement being entirely different. Using the parable of the mustard seed again, a comparison from the Gospel of Matthew, as set forth directly above, with the same story from the Gospel of Luke, set forth below, will provide an example:

Matthew 13:31–32 (RSV)	Luke: 13:18–19 (RSV)
Another parable he put before them, saying, "The kingdom of heaven is *like a grain of mustard seed which a man took and sowed in his* field; it is the smallest of all seed, but when it has grown it is the greatest of shrubs *and becomes a tree,* so that the *birds of the air* come and make *nests in its branches* (emphasis added)."	He said therefore, "What is the kingdom of God like? And to what shall I compare it: It is *like a grain of mustard seed which a man took and sowed in his* garden; and it grew *and became a tree,* and the *birds of the air* made *nests in its branches* (emphasis added)."

Only the italicized portions of the passage contain identical words. It is significant that the majority of phrases in passages like this fall within quotations of Jesus. Such a result would not be unexpected at a time when tradition required that those who followed a teacher would exercise extreme care in the transmission of those words to others, whether by memorization of oral teachings or by use of shorthand.

Another method of comparison calls on the most recent of twentieth-century developments, the computer and a program called "compare-write," in widespread use in the business world. It has the capability of comparing one document with another, word for word, highlighting identical words and phrases in the same sequence within the two documents (even where many additional, nonconforming words and phrases may appear in between the common identical words) and indicating deletions.

Every person who has used the compare-write program in drafting documents has had the experience of replacing a paragraph entirely with new and original language, using the same concepts and telling the same story, only to be surprised to find the same result as that set forth in the example above when the new document is finally printed out and compared to the old. Common experience, culture, and information will often create the result that groups of words will randomly appear in similar sequence in the new text, giving a false appearance that the second was actually *copied* from the first. The relevance of this type of comparison is therefore questionable in an analysis of originality.

The third type of comparison within the synoptic problem focuses upon identical, or almost identical, wording of entire sentences or passages. Because of the inconsistencies among modern translations evidenced above, it is probable that all of the so-called "identical passages" should really be considered within the preceding category type, not as a separate category of identical passages. Nevertheless, assuming the worst for the sake of argument and accepting the comparison made in the 1956 Throckmorton study, here is an example of identical passages:

Matthew 7:7–8 (RSV)	Luke 11:9–10 (RSV)
"Ask, and it will be given you; seek, and you will find; knock, and it will be opened to you. For every one who asks receives, and he who seeks finds, and to him who knocks it will be opened."	"Ask, and it will be given you; seek, and you will find; knock, and it will be opened to you. For every one who asks receives, and he who seeks finds, and to him who knocks it will be opened."

Again, it is relevant that the majority of these types of sentences or passages are quotations of Jesus. In a tradition that honored precise transmission of the words of teachers, quotations would have been routinely memorized, if not preserved in shorthand. The jury, however, must conclude for itself whether such passages that are assumed to be identical in precise wording actually exclude another explanation. The conclusion you reach will determine whether such testimony should be considered as original evidence given by only one witness (the originator), or whether it can be considered, for the reasons set forth above, as testimony given by the separate authors of the Gospels. Only those portions of the Gospels that are so alike as to force that conclusion should be placed into the category of being interdependent.

Based upon the foregoing, the first category of passages included by most biblical scholars within the so-called "synoptic problem," those with common themes but no identical wording, would clearly not be excluded as original evidence in a court of law. In fact, on the contrary, this testimony would have great credibility. Scholars who have contended that these passages were interdependent because of their similarity are simply incorrect under a legal analysis. The second category, containing common portions of passages, would reasonably be acceptable as evidence originating from two or more different witnesses who are otherwise credible, particularly where the similar language is contained within a quotation. This position is strengthened when the tradition of accuracy and precision of transmission of information so highly valued in the first century is considered.

Finally, if the jury determines that passages in the third category, containing longer portions of identical language, are deemed to be interdependent, then only one witness can be credited with originating that particular testimony. That determination will be made within the discretion of the jury, taking into consideration the credibility of the testimony as a whole as supported by corroborative evidence.

A review of the comparisons of all of the passages in these three Gospels is too extensive to present here. More important in reaching firm conclusions about our specific inquiry is the testimony presented in the Gospels of Matthew, Mark, and Luke regarding the crucifixion and resurrection of Jesus, beginning with events in the Garden of Gethsemane the night before the crucifixion of Jesus (Matt. 26:36; Mark 14:32; Luke 22:40). Again, using the 1956 Throckmorton study as a yardstick, an extremely small portion of this particular section of the Gospel of Luke is identical to the corresponding sections of Matthew and Mark. In the few portions of common text that do appear, only seven passages contain portions of substantially identical language.[14] Of these seven common passages, only three contain complete sentences, and even in this case some slight discrepancies still appear.

The jury may clearly conclude, therefore, that the Gospel of Luke is not dependent upon the Gospels of Mark and Matthew as to the limited facts we are analyzing and can be permitted to stand on its own as original testimony.

As noted above, the Gospel of Mark is significantly shorter than the Gospel of Matthew.[15] Assuming for the sake of argument that identical passages were in fact copied, from the beginning of events in the Garden of Gethsemane to the death of Jesus, more of Matthew appears to be original than Mark because of the extended narrative. The resurrection portion of the text appears to be entirely original in both Matthew and Mark, as in Luke. In the Gospels of Matthew and Mark, only minimal phrases exist in common regarding the resurrection of Jesus, and this similar text is essentially unimportant to the testimony.

Therefore, under a worst-case analysis of the Gospels of Matthew and Mark, the assertions of these two witnesses as to the actual crucifixion of Jesus could possibly, but not certainly, be viewed as partially interdependent. *Nevertheless, all three of the synoptic Gospels are clearly original and independent, prepared without concert, as to the portion of the testimony concerning the resurrection.* It is clear that each witness had his own perspective of the same event, which is not surprising because the Gospels report that they scattered after Jesus was arrested. In fact, the difference in perspective of the three witnesses, Matthew, Mark, and Luke, as well as that of John, becomes clearly evident when you recognize that the Gospel narratives are not presented in like chronological order, but rather are arranged by topics, according to the issues deemed to be important by the different writers.[16]

In his earlier treatise, Greenleaf concluded that the deviations between the Gospels of Mark and Matthew—and we could add to that the Gospel of Luke—in the order of time, in arrangement of facts, and the inclusion of matters in each that do not appear in the other, show that as a whole they cannot be mere copies of each other, and it is likely that no one is the source for the other.[17] The jury is entitled to determine the impact of the commonality of these three Gospels upon an analysis of the Gospels as evidence in our case.

Notwithstanding all of this, taking into consideration both the similarities and the variations, each of the four Gospels is consistent and original in the testimony that Jesus died on the cross for his refusal to repudiate his own divinity, as described in the teachings set forth in those Gospels, and that he rose from the dead on the third day, counting the day of his death as the first day.

CHAPTER FIVE

Credibility—Character and Consistency

W e have established that the four Gospel testimonies were written by Matthew, Mark, Luke, and John approximately two thousand years ago, close to the time the actual events occurred. Having established that under the rules of evidence applicable in a federal court the Gospels will in fact be admissible for the jury to consider, and the opportunity for firsthand observation that the witnesses had, we now move forward to review the value of the evidence to prove, or not prove, our case. We know that, if the Gospel testimony can be shown to be credible, we will have established as historical fact that a person named Jesus lived two thousand years ago as described in the Gospels, died on the cross, and three days later returned to life.

Let us then turn to the probative value of the manuscript evidence of the four Gospels—that is, the tendency of the evidence to establish, or prove, the proposition for which it is offered. Because these are facts that were cognizable by the senses of our witnesses, the value of this testimony depends at this stage of our analysis primarily upon the *credibility* of the witnesses themselves. The issue to be examined now is whether or not the statements made by the authors of the Gospels are truthful. To find out we will first review the character, or the reliability, of the witnesses themselves. We will begin by assuming the burden of our missing opponents to examine the character of the witnesses for truthfulness or untruthfulness, a process ordinarily provided in a cross-examination. The evidence must also be measured against our ordinary experience and expectations. Second, we will test the facts and circumstances surrounding the details of the testimony to determine whether that collateral evidence tends to corroborate what the witnesses have said.

As you will recall, the traditional standard by which we are required to prove our case in a federal court is proof by a preponderance of the evidence. That is, the evidence must lead you, the jury, to find that the existence of the contested fact is more probable than its nonexistence. If the evidence is such that a reasonable person could not help but draw an inference that the fact is true, then the court will *require* a verdict in favor of the proponent of the fact.[1]

In his nineteenth-century treatise, Greenleaf established a five-part test for determining credibility, taken from the general common law of his time prior to enactment of the Federal Rules of Evidence. This test is still useful to order our examination of the witnesses themselves and of the related facts, to determine the credence to which the authors of the Gospels are entitled as witnesses in a court of law. Greenleaf found that the credibility of these witnesses depends, *first,* upon their honesty; *second,* upon their ability; *third,* on the number of witnesses and the consistency of their testimony; *fourth,* on the conformity of the testimony with experience; and *fifth,* on the coincidence of their testimony with collateral facts and circumstances.[2] The objective is to determine the accuracy of the perception, recordation, recollection, and sincerity of the witness.[3]

It is not necessary under our system of law for each item of evidence to stand on its own as proof of the issue that we are examining. Evidence is introduced to the jury item by item, with each item of evidence creating a link in the entire chain of proof, to build the case cumulatively. It is enough with each item of evidence that it reasonably shows that a fact is slightly more probable than it would appear without the evidence. As we have recognized previously, the jury may consider both direct and circumstantial evidence.

The *first* element of the Greenleaf credibility test requires an examination of the honesty of the authors of the Gospels. There is an initial presumption of truth given to witnesses. This is bolstered, however, by our own knowledge that the early dating of the Gospels implies that many of the people who were present at the events reported would have also been people who received the Gospels. The narratives include recent experiences of the very people who were exposed to the Gospels at the time. These members of the community, therefore, provided a natural monitor of the honesty and related accuracy of the witnesses. If the Gospels were false in their assertions, the teachings would not have been so widely accepted without criticism. In this regard, it is clear that accuracy was important to the authors, and statements to that effect in the Gospels indicate that the authors understood that accuracy was also important to readers in the community at that time.

As an expert on the laws of evidence, Greenleaf noted that the use of the authentication of credentials in the New Testament indicated a recognition by the authors that the communities for whom the Gospels were written placed a premium on accurate testimony. The high value placed upon precision of transmission of information in the Jewish community was indicated by customs established hundreds of years before the first century, and that priority continued during and after the time the Gospels were written and had begun to be circulated. Because precision in memorization of important texts and teachings was considered to be a sacred task, there is no reason to assume that any of our witnesses involved in transmission of this information in the community at the time that the Gospels were written would not be accurate, or would create false traditions, particularly where other living witnesses to the events were available to provide immediate criticism.

Likewise, it is clear that the authors of the Gospels understood what they were writing. The use of allegories and metaphors was customary in the first century, but the statements regarding the death and resurrection of Jesus in the Gospels are given as mere facts. There is no reason to believe that people living in those communities were not aware of the difference between empirical facts on the one hand and myths and metaphors on the other. That people living in the first century understood this distinction is revealed by the use of the word *mythos* in several New Testament books (see 1 Tim. 1:4; 4:7; 2 Tim. 4:4; Titus 1:14; 2 Pet. 1:16). Followers of the Gospel teachings were admonished not to be deceived by "myths," "worldly fables," "speculation," and "cleverly devised tales."

Remember that in connection with our preliminary authentication of the Gospel testimony, evidence to rebut the question of motive or incentive to falsify the testimony was introduced to the jury. The authors of the Gospels would have been totally without honor to create such a falsehood and to teach it to others who would clearly endure such suffering as a result of the belief. Such behavior would be completely inconsistent with the character of the apostles so far as has been historically established from their conduct and the nature of their teachings.

While the disciples have not been presented in the Gospels as being of particularly strong character prior to the resurrection, subsequently they became strong leaders of the new church, willing to die for their convictions. The change in the lives of the apostles, including particularly Matthew, Peter, and John, was significant after the resurrection. For example, the night that Jesus was taken by soldiers to face a mock trial, Peter, the true author of the Gospel of Mark, reported against his own interest that he in cowardice had three times denied even knowing Jesus. It is a historical fact that after the resurrection Peter was completely transformed and preached the Gospel publicly at a time when this was punishable by death.[4] Tradition holds that Peter was crucified upside down in Nero's circus in Rome, around A.D. 64. Today, excavations have shown that St. Peter's Basilica in Rome is built upon a first-century cemetery, and the Roman Catholic Church has taken the official position that it marks the grave of Peter.[5]

Because the testimony of the Gospels rests directly upon the observation and truthfulness of our four principal witnesses—Matthew, Mark, Luke, and John—the nature of the character of those witnesses is critically material to the case. Where the character of the witnesses bears on credibility and is an essential element of the case, as a test of the reliability of the witnesses the court will permit and in fact will encourage evidence of their specific conduct as proof of character.[6]

> *In cases in which character or a trait of character of*
> *a person is an essential element of a charge, claim or*
> *defense, proof may also be made of specific instances*
> *of that person's conduct.*[7]

Additionally, as we are assuming somewhat the burden of cross-examination of the character of the witnesses, it is relevant to note that the court will have discretion to permit the use of extrinsic evidence such as the conduct of people in the community in such a cross-examination if it tends to show or disprove the truthfulness or untruthfulness of the witnesses.[8]

Whether or not we believe that the events reported by the authors of the four Gospels are true, it is clear from their own conduct, by the fact that they were willing to suffer for the rest of their lives and even to die for the right to teach that these events occurred, that they were truthful in their testimony at least insofar as they did *believe it to be true*. People do not die for what they *know* to be untrue—for a lie.

Additionally, it is also clear from the conduct of other followers of Jesus that people in the community at the time the events occurred also believed that the Gospel testimony reported facts that were true. Their own intense belief was founded upon those facts. All the followers of Jesus suffered extensively; they lost families and friends, property, status, and many of them died excruciating deaths rather than recant their belief. None of them became rich and none of them gained political power by following the teaching of the Gospels. Under the law, assertions may be communicated through conduct, as well as by words. The conduct of those who received the teachings of the Gospels from our four witnesses reflects their opinion that these witnesses were honest and trustworthy. In fact, with respect to assertions made in ancient documents, courts have held that the conduct of others demonstrating reliance upon such assertions is strong evidence concerning such matters.[9]

The Federal Rules of Evidence permit the jury to consider as evidence opinion testimony as to the character or a trait of character of the authors of the Gospels.[10] The people who lived in the community in which Jesus and our principal witnesses lived, and those who received the teachings of the Gospels from Matthew, Mark, Luke, or John, are also witnesses in our case. They are no longer able to speak directly to us, but through their conduct they have offered their opinions that these were honest and honorable people.

For example, Ignatius was believed to have known the apostle John. Ignatius was torn apart by wild animals for his belief in the truth of the Gospel testimony. In A.D. 115, in the face of certain death, when he could have saved himself by repudiation, he wrote the following about Jesus:

> He was crucified and died under Pontius Pilate. He
> really, and not merely in appearance, was crucified,
> and died, in the sight of beings in heaven, and on

earth, and under the earth . . . He also rose again in
three days . . . On the day of the preparation, then,
at the third hour, He received the sentence from
Pilate, the Father permitting that to happen; at the
sixth hour He was crucified; at the ninth hour He
gave up the ghost; and before sunset He was buried.
During the Sabbath He continued under the earth in
the tomb in which Joseph of Arimathea had laid Him
. . . at the dawning of the Lord's day he arose from
the dead, according to what was spoken by
Himself.[11]

This statement directly reflects the teaching of the Gospels and
the belief that was instilled in the followers of that teaching. A
statement such as this, referred to as a "dying declaration," is
given great weight under the law since the declarant was conscious that death was near and certain at the time that the statement was made. It is important to recognize that Ignatius was
fully aware of his pending death at this time. In the same letter
he acknowledged that if the resurrection were not a fact, then
his appointed death in the arena would be "in vain" and he
would be guilty of falsehood.[12] This statement therefore evinces
the absolute conviction of Ignatius regarding his belief in the
truth of the testimony of the Gospels and the resurrection of
Jesus. The principle upon which the credibility granted to a
dying declaration is based was stated as early as 1789:

When the party is at the point of death, when every
hope of this world is gone, when every motive to
falsehood is silenced and the mind is induced by the
most powerful considerations to speak the truth; a
situation so solemn, and so awful, is considered by

the law as creating an obligation equal to that which is imposed by a positive oath administered in a Court of Justice.[13]

Is it reasonable to suppose that a belief so strong, so deep, so intense, could have its basis in a lie deliberately delivered to the entire community by four different witnesses—witnesses with significant corroborating evidence to support their testimony? It is clear that the communities in which these witnesses lived and taught believed that the four authors of the Gospels were truthful, and their conduct ratified that belief. The logical inference is that it is impossible to read about the conduct and the lives of the authors of the Gospels, as well as the lives of the remaining apostles and the people who received their messages, and conclude that their lives were without honor, or that their actions were based upon untruthfulness.

In summary, respecting this first test of credibility, the reports in the Gospels indicate a lack of artifice. They are written in a most believable way, simply and without embellishment. In addition, the conduct of the four principal witnesses, and of the communities in which they lived and taught, reflects the simple honesty of the testimony. Greenleaf summarized the factors that would induce a jurist to accept the testimony of these four witnesses as being the simplicity of the narratives, the absence of a sense of self-importance or any anxiety to be believed or impress others, and the lack of drama in the description of the events. In fact, the narratives are written as if they are recording events well known to the public in their own country and time. The authors give us no sense of concern that they will not be believed or that they have to be convincing. They evidence a complete disassociation with any particular agenda. And the conduct of the community in response to that testimony reflects a consensus that the witnesses were honest and truthful.

The *second* element of the credibility test is the ability of the witness to tell the truth. Greenleaf pointed out that this depends upon the opportunities that the witness has had to observe the facts, the accuracy of discernment, and memory.[14] We have already examined the opportunity each author of the Gospels had to observe the circumstances at first hand. Additionally, particularly taking into account the recent redating of the Gospels, under the law we are not required to accept speculation by critics that recollections of the authors were distorted by the passage of time.

The Federal Rules of Evidence provide that:

Every person is competent to be a witness except as otherwise provided in these rules.[15]

For our case, the rules do not provide otherwise.

Although we know nothing about their actual memory capability, Greenleaf concluded that the four Gospel writers are entitled to a presumption under the law that they were capable and of sound mind, with an average or ordinary degree of intelligence.[16] In particular, Greenleaf noted that the detail given in their testimony as well as their own histories also supports this presumption of sound mind and intelligence. But let us examine each one individually as to ability or capability.

As a tax collector for the Roman administration in Palestine, Matthew would have been familiar with the customs and procedures of that system and of the community in which he worked, though he would not have necessarily been recognized as a scholar. During this period Rome was establishing its domination over Judea. Herod Antipas, the appointed Roman ruler of Galilee between A.D. 4 and A.D. 39, imposed heavy taxes on the people in the area in which Matthew lived.[17] Numerous taxes are known to have been imposed at varying rates—customs duty on merchandise, tariffs, a capitation tax, and a land tax, among others. It would be unusual to find that they were paid voluntarily with no discontent, evasion, or fraud, and it is reasonable to assume that a person with the responsibility for collecting these taxes would have had to understand and deal with those circumstances.

It is reasonable to assume that Matthew, as a tax collector, was vigilant, suspicious, and careful by nature. Matthew would not have been easy to deceive. He would not have been naive as a witness, and his testimony should be viewed in this context.

Other books of the New Testament and writings of the early church fathers indicate that Mark traveled throughout the Roman Empire to teach the gospel with Paul and Barnabas, and tradition holds that he later visited Paul in Rome. Subsequently he traveled with Peter in Asia before returning to Rome. Mark was therefore an experienced traveler with a broader exposure to different cultures than the average person residing in Judea at that time. The Latin phrases contained in this Gospel indicate a higher level of education. Evidence offered for consideration by the jury in the next chapter will show that the facts and references recited by Mark are historically accurate, underscoring the precision and correct manner of his reporting.

As mentioned above, Luke is believed to have been a physician. He was a very accurate observer, and his Gospel indicates that he paid particular attention to Jesus' power to heal. For example, in the Gospel of Luke a woman is described as being "in the grip of a major fever." The language specifically reflects Greek first-century medical terminology for someone afflicted with a major illness. During that period medical writers described fevers as divided into major and minor classes.[18] Greenleaf has observed that while Matthew and Mark described a man healed by Jesus as a leper, Luke describes him as being "full of leprosy." While the other writers describe a withered hand, Luke more precisely describes the man as having a right hand that is withered.

Luke introduced a psychological aspect into the testimony of his Gospel by suggesting that the sleep of the apostles in the Garden of Gethsemane the night before Jesus was taken away by soldiers was induced by a state of extreme sorrow. Luke also mentioned that, on the same night in the garden, the agony of Jesus, who knew what was to come, caused his sweat to become "like drops of blood, falling down upon the ground" (Luke 22:44). Medical experts today know that this apparent sweating of blood resembles a medical condition triggered by extreme stress called hematidrosis, which causes subcutaneous blood vessels to rupture into the exocrine sweat glands.[19]

Luke also pictured the character of Jesus in a very detailed way. This Gospel indicates Jesus' familiarity with country life consistent with what we know today about the rural town of Nazareth where he grew up. Luke has described the knowledge that Jesus showed about how to revive a barren fig tree, farm animals' need for watering, the amount of yeast necessary to leaven dough, and the mother hen's gathering and protection of her chicks.[20] Recent archaeological findings in the ancient village of Nazareth, discussed below, corroborate Luke's testimony by establishing the rural and agricultural nature of the town, despite its close proximity to more sophisticated cities.

Luke carefully placed the events that he reported within a historical context, and these historical references have been verified. For example, when writing of the birth of Jesus, Luke established the date by reference to Jesus' birth during Herod's reign while Quirinius was governor of Syria, at a time when a decree requiring a census had been issued by Caesar Augustus (Luke 2:1, 2). The writings of Josephus reported the Roman census as having occurred in A.D. 6; because of this Luke was first believed to be incorrect. Luke's historical references have recently been proven accurate by archaeologists and historians. It has now been determined that the census procedure was begun prior to the birth of Jesus during the reign of the emperor Augustus. Additionally, an inscription has been found in Antioch that described Quirinius as holding a position of authority in Syria at that time.[21] A papyrus found in Egypt verifies the existence of a law that required everyone to return to their initial homes for the census, as described in Luke's narrative of the return of Joseph and Mary to Bethlehem.[22]

Critics of the Gospel of John have generally described the apostle John as a humble fisherman and have wondered how he could have written so eloquently. Several discoveries now offer a greater understanding of the social and political changes occurring in the region at that time. Inhabitants of Galilee were not mere provincials. It is known that no town or village in any part of Galilee was more than fifteen miles from a major city. Excavations from the period show a clear transition in the culture; for example, cash crops began to replace subsistence farming. The entire area was greatly influenced by the Roman culture.[23]

In 1986, during a period of drought, the waters of the Sea of Galilee receded, revealing a fishing boat in the mud, five miles east of the location of the town of Capernaum where John lived.[24] It is the first ancient boat to have been discovered in this area, and it has now been excavated and preserved. Radiocarbon dating of the wood assigns a date for this boat between A.D. 20 and A.D. 40, exactly the time of the Gospel events.

The excavated boat is very similar to the type of vessel that is described in the Gospels as having been used by John and his father for fishing. It is twenty-six and one-half feet long, seven and one-half feet wide and four and one-half feet high, with a large platform-shaped stern. It could be sailed as well as rowed and would have needed a crew of at least five.[25] If John's father owned a boat like this, he would have had to hire employees. In fact, the Gospel of Mark recites that John and his father had "hired servants" (Mark 1:20). Additionally, the boat would have been fit to carry substantial cargo. It is clear that the family of John was of at least moderate substance. There is no reason to believe that John was so humble as to be incapable of writing this Gospel.

John was also perceptive in his reporting. He depicted the harmony between the nature of Jesus and country life that was described by Luke as well. In various passages of this Gospel, Jesus is reported as having referred to himself as a "shepherd" whose followers knew his voice, as sheep know the voice of their shepherd. In Palestine, sheep lived with one shepherd for many years because they were traditionally raised for wool, not food. The sheep learned to trust and love their shepherds. The writer William Barclay has described many examples of this bond, which Jesus recognized. For example, a flock of sheep housed with other flocks in a common shelter can be separated from the others merely by a call from the shepherd. The flock will run to their own shepherd because they recognize the voice.[26]

The Gospel of John gains credence by the many detailed and accurate references in the manner of a familiar observer to geographical features of Jerusalem and the surrounding area that existed only prior to its destruction in A.D. 70. Some examples of these have already been introduced to the jury. In addition to the evidentiary value this has to the early dating of that Gospel, the accuracy of his reporting of these details has been verified by many other archaeological discoveries that we will examine soon, as well as by the writings of other historians.

As to the *third* element of Greenleaf's credibility test, we must analyze the "number of witnesses" and the "consistency" of the testimonies of the authors of the four Gospels. With respect to the nonconforming portions of the Gospels, they are all consistent as to material facts, and they all corroborate each other. For example, Greenleaf noted that the character of Jesus as portrayed by the four Gospel writers is perfectly consistent, which is particularly convincing given the unusual nature of Jesus.[27] Additionally, Greenleaf has pointed out that, as one would ordinarily expect with truthful witnesses, the integrity of the testimony is confirmed by the fact that there is enough discrepancy among the Gospels to show that they were all independent narrators of those events.[28] Many scholars have shown throughout the years that discrepancies between the details of the four Gospels are not sufficient to invalidate their testimony, and there are no contradictions on the fundamental points. Differences between the Gospel narratives can be harmonized.

Taking into consideration the so-called "synoptic problem" so far as the consistency test is concerned, evidence has established that the identity of passages that do exist in the portion of each Gospel describing the crucifixion and resurrection of Jesus has minimal impact. The synoptic analysis has not diminished the corroborative value of the Gospels regarding the facts of the resurrection of Jesus. With respect to our particular issue—that is, the truth of the life, death, and resurrection of Jesus—though there are differences in the telling of the events, there is no deviation among the Gospels as to the fact that these events occurred, and the evidence does not sustain an argument that the resurrection passages were copied among any of the Gospels.

The *fourth* element of the credibility test, comparing the "conformity of the testimony with experience," requires us to consider scientific evidence that has come to light in the last few decades of the twentieth century and to use it to judge the Gospel testimony against our own experiences. In the nineteenth century when Greenleaf first addressed this issue, he stated that he believed that this element of the credibility test presented the more difficult problem under strict legal scrutiny because the resurrection of Jesus and the miracles related by the Gospels are not ordinary events that others can relate to their own experiences. But Greenleaf did not have the benefit of modern scientific information available to us today.

When weighing testimony against our own experience, the jury must be careful not to base judgments of events merely upon personal knowledge, because this excludes information that we can obtain through a process of inductive or deductive reasoning, without which there will be no advancement of knowledge. For that reason, the law permits us to reasonably infer other facts from what we do see and know or understand.

The scientific process relies on the same reasoning, and that is how it advances knowledge. For example, mathematical proofs are often based upon propositions or axioms that are merely *assumed* to be true for the sake of studying the consequences. Following the protocol utilized in science, the jury should not reject evidence of a fact such as the resurrection merely because it requires an assumption based on the unknown. The interesting development of mathematical models that form the basis for new hypotheses in physics as well as in mathematics would not be possible without the use of such assumptions. This is reasoning based on the unknown. We reason and infer conclusions from those assumptions. Godel's famous "incompleteness" theorem recognizes that certain systems of proof used to advance knowledge will always utilize such assumptions that are unprovable, or unknowable, under the rules used by that system.[29] In fact, the very *process* of thinking is not yet understood. The British mathematician Roger Penrose has concluded that the insight required by mathematical reasoning and any other system of logic is intuitive and lies beyond mere computational, or formalized, rules.[30]

Daily we accept things that we do not understand. Today many scientists studying human consciousness have recognized that conscious activity and the ability to reason beyond the mere processing and computation of information transcends the physical ability of the brain. Even our ability to perceive and enjoy simple things such as the color red, or the smell of a rose, or happiness and love, is not understood. Science does not explain how a physical system like the human brain can give rise to these types of conscious experiences. This nonphysical aspect of consciousness awareness, like the resurrection, currently has no scientific explanation.[31]

Today it is common protocol for scientists to accept the existence of facts and circumstances without understanding the related cause. For example, astrophysicists have provided convincing evidence that the universe is finite—it had a beginning and it will have an end. The model of the creation of the universe established by the Big Bang Theory as it is now accepted by most scientists holds that all matter, energy, space, and time began with an explosion from a point much smaller than the period at the end of this sentence. Because of the compelling evidence upon which this theory is based, many scientists have now concluded that the beginning and end of the universe form boundaries to space-time, and these are the boundaries at which the laws of science break down.[32]

Simply put, the scientists hold that not only matter, but also time as we know it, began with this large explosion from a single tiny point. Since we know that every event must have a cause, reason requires that the first cause of the universe occurred outside of matter, time, and space as we know it. That cause, therefore, could not have been governed by, and would not be limited by, our known natural laws. We could refer to this cause as being supernatural, or we could refer to it as existing in another dimension of matter, time, and space. The only alternative to this conclusion under current scientific understanding is to hypothesize that the creation event had no cause at all, a theory that is explored by scientists predisposed to question the very foundation for religious belief, but a hypothesis that is speculative at best.[33] One thing is clear, however; from the point of view of science, the first cause of our universe is not yet understood.

Likewise, it is important to consider that in the study of the origin of life, we have been willing to accept the existence of many fundamental physical facts without understanding the cause. No empirical scientific explanation for the origin of life has ever been published. Dr. Hubert P. Yockey, in a text written for researchers dealing with molecular evolution, used the science of information theory and coding theory in molecular biology to conclude that "the origin of life by chance in a primeval soup is impossible in probability in the same way that a perpetual motion machine is impossible in probability . . . . A practical person must conclude that life didn't happen by chance."[34]

In fact, Yockey has noted that there is absolutely no evidence independent of the existence of life even to support the hypothesis for a primeval soup with the building blocks of life, even though the existence of such a circumstance is the foundation for all origin of life research.[35] The conclusion of a careful summary and analysis of the current status of laboratory and theoretical research on the origins-of-life is that it is not likely that life on earth could have begun spontaneously by purely chemical and physical means, and, in fact, such studies appear to have reached an impasse.[36]

The closest that we have ever come to demonstrating how life could have originated by natural processes is the well-known Miller-Urey electrical sparking type of experiment in which very small quantities of only a few amino acids were produced, along with tar. That is a long way from the creation of life. A special set of twenty amino acids are used by living cells to construct proteins, but proteins are only one of the building blocks that make up a bacterial cell (one of the smallest and simplest forms of life).[37] The Miller-Urey type of experiment is still typical of the best chemistry produced in any laboratory on the origin of life, but experts acknowledge that creating a few amino acids does not come close to achieving a living organism. In fact, it has been stated that these amino acids "no more resemble a bacterium than a small pile of real and nonsense words, each written on an individual scrap of paper, resembles the complete works of Shakespeare."[38]

What has emerged in recent work from experimentation on the possibility of chemical evolution on a random, undirected basis (that is, the earliest stage of evolution in which the very earliest living things came into being) appears to be an alternative scenario of destruction of life under primitive conditions rather than the synthesis of life.[39] Again, like the mystery of the resurrection, our experience is that the origins of life are "unknowables" under our current scientific understanding.

Furthermore, new research on understanding of microsystems—for example, the biological systems at the cellular level within living organisms, such as the human vision system, the immune system, or the blood clotting system—shows that not only the origin but also the evolution of many of those systems cannot be explained by present scientific knowledge. In other words, these subcellular systems are "irreducibly complex" in that each part of the whole is completely dependent at all times upon the existence of the hundreds of other parts in the system. For that reason their internal development cannot be explained by numerous, successive slight modifications.[40] That lack of understanding does not stop scientists from studying the systems.

Scientists have also shown that things exist within our universe that cannot be perceived by ordinary sensory mechanisms. In fact, scientists currently accept that an enormous percentage of the mass in the universe is composed of cold, dark matter that we cannot see or touch, and that can be measured only through circumstantial evidence.[41] Quantum physics, which deals with particles that are infinitely small and ordinarily cannot be seen, is fundamentally based upon acceptance of the unknown and unknowable, and that is why principles such as Heisenberg's "uncertainty principle"[42] are uniformly accepted and integrated into research and conclusions in quantum physics. For example, neutrinos are ghostly particles—only rarely detected through circumstantial evidence—that have been demonstrated to have the ability to "pass through six trillion miles of lead without leaving any trace of its passage."[43]

Additionally, scientists now routinely accept that primordial black holes exist, based solely upon circumstantial evidence, deductions from principles such as the effect of gravity on light.[44] A black hole is a region of space in which matter is so concentrated and the pull of its gravity is so powerful that nothing, not even light, can emerge from it; it has been described as a whirling vortex around an ultimate point of no return. It can only be detected through indirect evidence.[45] As you can see, therefore, the use of inductive and deductive reasoning based upon indirect circumstantial evidence to test the credibility of testimony regarding an event, or the cause of an event, is acceptable in science as well as in a court of law.

Science has already accepted the hypothesis that physical facts, or events, may exist without an understanding of their physical causes. Similarly, lack of understanding of the physical cause is not a reason to reject the testimony of the authors of the Gospels if the evidence appears otherwise credible. If we can accept the basic premise that even one physical event can occur in this universe without an understanding of the cause, then we cannot rule out testimony by the four Gospel witnesses that other such events with inexplicable causes occurred merely because we do not understand them.

Even in the nineteenth century, while acknowledging that ordinary experience of each reader of the Gospels compelled special scrutiny, Greenleaf concluded that if these events were "separately testified to by different witnesses of ordinary intelligence and integrity, in any court of justice, the jury would be bound to believe them; and a verdict, rendered contrary to the uncontradicted testimony of credible witnesses to any of these plain facts, separately taken, would be liable to be set aside, as a verdict against evidence."[46] Today, as science and history have advanced, the inexplicable and the unknowable have become a part of our everyday personal experience. As required under the fourth element of the credibility test, the life, death, and resurrection of Jesus are not inconsistent with the jury's experience.

In summary, the testimony of the four witnesses as preserved in the Gospels has met the first four elements of the credibility test established by Greenleaf, an eminent authority on the rules of evidence. The evidence is sufficient to support a finding of honesty, ability, consistency with the testimony of the other witnesses, and the conformity of the testimony with our own experience and expectations.

CHAPTER SIX

Credibility—Collateral Circumstances and Corroboration

T he *fifth* element of the credibility test, "the coincidence of their testimony with collateral facts and circumstances," requires a comparison of the details of the various reports of the Gospels with other known historical facts, including details of circumstances provided by other witnesses, to see if they are consistent with the testimony. This is a very important test of veracity because it is difficult for people to invent stories and keep all of the details of the circumstances harmonious with the facts of the story. Nothing happens in a vacuum; everything happens in relation to other people and the things and events occurring around them. This is why a "false witness" usually tries to deal with general statements and broad assertions rather than detailing circumstances against which the testimony might later be contradicted. For that reason, variety and minuteness of detail are generally regarded as tests of sincerity.[1]

Even where a false witness does give details, the testimony is often only detailed as to the portions that have been prepared. Beyond that point it will become vague and general. In other words, the testimony will not be uniform in texture; an untruthful witness will remember some things in great detail and won't be able to recall others. A truthful witness is visibly natural and unaffected in his or her testimony and will recite details evenly in every part of the narrative.[2]

Usually false testimony is revealed by inconsistencies in the details and surrounding circumstances related by other witnesses. A search for corroborating evidence, therefore, is usually a search for circumstantial evidence.

> *The increased number of witnesses to circumstances, and the increased number of the circumstances themselves, all tend to increase the probability of detection if the witnesses are false . . . Thus the force of circumstantial evidence is found to depend on the number of particulars involved in the narrative; the difficulty of fabricating them all, if false, and the great facility of detection; the nature of the circumstances to be compared, and from which the dates and other facts are to be collected; the intricacy of the comparison; the number of the intermediate steps in the process of deduction; and the circuity of the investigation. The more largely the narrative partakes of these characters, the further it will be found removed from all suspicion of contrivance or design,*

*and the more profoundly the mind will repose on the
conviction of its truth.*[3]

As an expert on the law of evidence, Greenleaf believed in
the nineteenth century that the evidence supporting the facts of
the Gospels was sufficient to lead us to a certainty that these
events occurred. If this type of circumstantial evidence is sufficient to convict a person of a crime and cause that person to be
incarcerated, or even put to death, surely it ought to be considered sufficient to determine our acceptance of the evidence put
forth in the narratives of the Gospels.

We must treat the evidence presented in the Gospels as we
would treat the evidence of other matters. The witnesses must
be compared for credibility with themselves and each other,
with surrounding facts and circumstances; and their testimony
must be tested against the evidence presented by the adverse
parties.

Ancient writers, archaeological findings, conclusions of scientists, medical opinions, and artifacts that have been preserved
through the years have all been found to confirm the details of
the accounts presented in the Gospels. In many cases events that
at first appeared to be somewhat inconsistent or contradictory
have been proven true through recent discoveries. In fact, substantially all of the factual statements in the Gospels that provide context, or a frame of reference historically, have been verified by empirical evidence.

For example, the Gospel writers described governmental
authorities and existing manners and customs of the times and
places in which they lived in minute and precise detail that can
be, and in most cases has been, verified by history and archaeology. The historical details do not have the appearance of

contrivance or design, but are scattered evenly and naturally throughout every part of each of the narratives. Each incident connects with every other incident in a way that makes falsehood impossible.

It is important to consider also that all four Gospels contain this minuteness and scope of detail even though the authors wrote at different times and in different places. They all refer incidentally to the same collateral facts and to the same general circumstances. Although there are some discrepancies in their testimony, this is no more than one would expect from four different witnesses, each testifying from his or her own perspective.

When analyzing the consistency of the details of the circumstances reported in the four Gospels, the jury should recognize that during that period the entire region had been incorporated into the Roman Empire, undergoing tremendous political and governmental turmoil. In A.D. 4, Rome annexed Judea, causing political unrest throughout the territory that actually culminated in the revolt against Rome approximately sixty-four years later.

The local and regional governments and rulers were constantly changing, with various parts of the area being controlled by many different authorities. Confusing laws and regulations for the administration of justice existed in all parts of the territory. It would be hard to identify any place or period in history more difficult to describe consistently when referring to circumstances surrounding an event. For example, details such as who was in charge, what customs prevailed at the time the event occurred, or what legal procedures were required for the trial of Jesus would have been hard to fabricate.[4] If the testimony were falsified, it would also have been inconsistent. Contradictory details surrounding fundamental points would have given opponents every opportunity to discredit the testimony publicly. This Gospel testimony can now be effectively cross-examined by comparing it to known historical facts and verifiable evidence. Greenleaf illustrated this type of analysis with regard to the trial of Jesus prior to his crucifixion:

> They brought him to Pontius Pilate. We know both from Tacitus and Josephus [two historians of the time], that he was at that time governor of Judea. A sentence from him was necessary before they could proceed to the execution of Jesus; and we know that the power of life and death was usually vested in the Roman governor. [Jesus] was treated with derision; and this we know to have been a customary practice at that time, previous to the execution of criminals, and during the time of it. Pilate scourged Jesus before he gave him up to be crucified. We know from ancient authors, that this was a very usual practice among Romans. The accounts of an execution generally run in this form: he was stripped, whipped, and beheaded or executed. According to the evangelists, his accusation was written on the top of the cross; and we learn from Suetonius and others, that the crime of the person to be executed was affixed to the instrument of his punishment. According to the evangelists, this accusation was written in three different languages; and we know from Josephus that it was quite common in Jerusalem to have all public advertisements written in this manner. According to the

evangelists, Jesus had to bear his cross; and we know from other sources of information, that this was the constant practice of these times. According to the evangelists, the body of Jesus was given up to be buried at the request of a friend. We know that, unless the criminal was infamous, this was the law or the custom with all Roman governors.[5]

Since the time of that analysis, particularly within the past few decades, much more historical, archaeological and other empirical evidence has been discovered to corroborate the credibility of the Gospel reports. Let us first review what evidence in the form of historical writing is available to substantiate the fact that Jesus was a real person, that he actually lived two thousand years ago, and that he was crucified on the cross. We have already reviewed many of the historical references to the actual existence of Jesus by ancient writers, including those other than Christian writers. In addition, many other contemporary, or near contemporary, first- and second-century writers have made historical references to the actual existence of Jesus or have corroborated facts about his life as reported in the Gospels.

Tacitus, an early Roman historian who lived between A.D. 60 and A.D. 120, referred to the fact that Nero put many Christians to death whose "Chrestus, from whom their name was derived, was executed at the hands of the procurator Pontius Pilatus in the reign of Tiberius."[6] Suetonius, a contemporary of Tacitus, referred to Jews who were "continually making disturbances at the instigation of Crestus" so that the emperor Claudius expelled them from Rome.[7] The reference to "Chrestus" or "Crestus" is generally accepted by scholars as a reference to Jesus, as Christ. Pliny (the Younger), governor of Bithynia, wrote to Trajan in A.D. 112 to report that his test for persons accused of being a Christian was to make them curse Christ, which a genuine Christian cannot be induced to do.[8] After an investigation of Christians, he had determined that they were accustomed to meet at daybreak and sing hymns to Christus, as God.[9] None of these writers was Christian.

In approximately A.D. 52, a historian, Thallus, wrote a history of the eastern Mediterranean area. Although the work has been lost, fragments of his words have been preserved in references by other ancient scholars. Julius Africanus reported in A.D. 221 that Thallus had written in A.D. 52 of the crucifixion of Jesus. The Gospel of Luke states that as Jesus died upon the cross "darkness fell over the whole land" (Luke 23:44). Africanus reported that Thallus described this event as an eclipse of the sun, which Africanus believed to be an unlikely explanation because the moon was full at the time of the Jewish Passover season when Jesus died, and an eclipse could not take place during the time of the full moon.[10]

The great ancient books written by Josephus, *Wars of the Jews* and *Antiquities of the Jews,* contain numerous contemporary historical details that have been confirmed by archaeological discoveries. The writings of Josephus, which survive in copies, are the primary sources of information regarding the Jewish people and their history, customs, and manners during the time of Jesus. Josephus clearly referred to the fact of the actual existence of Jesus in the following famous passage:

> Now, there was about this time, Jesus, a wise man, if
> it be lawful to call him a man, for he was a doer of
> wonderful works,—a teacher of such men as receive

the truth with pleasure. He drew over to him both many of the Jews and many of the Gentiles. He was [the] Christ; and when Pilate, at the suggestion of the principal men amongst us, had condemned him to the cross, those that loved him at the first, did not forsake him, for he appeared to them alive again the third day, as the divine prophets had foretold these and ten thousand other wonderful things concerning him; and the tribe of Christians, so named from him, are not extinct at this day.[11]

The particular wording of this passage has created much controversy because a reference to Jesus as "the Christ" was considered to be unlikely since Josephus was not a Christian. For that reason, though the passage as a whole is not generally questioned, speculation is that the references to Jesus as a Messiah were added by later Christian writers. The suspected revision to the text is supported by the fact that Origen, who lived from A.D. 185 to A.D. 254, stated that Josephus did not refer to Jesus as the Christ. Scholars believe that they have reconstructed the original language, and that the unadulterated passage referred specifically and clearly to the crucifixion of Jesus, without referring to him as the Messiah.

On the other hand, a tenth-century Arabic manuscript published in the early 1970s described the substance of the same passage as including the original reference to Jesus as "perhaps the Messiah."[12] Since the Arabic text would not be as vulnerable to an argument that it was tampered with by Christian writers, it has the "earmark of authenticity," and it is possible that the original statement by Josephus did in fact contain that reference.[13]

Later in the same *Antiquities,* Josephus also referred to James as the brother of Jesus. The passage states that the high priest, Annas, acting without proper authority, assembled the Sanhedrin and "brought before them the brother of Jesus, who was called the Christ, whose name was James, and some others [or some of his companions]; and when he had formed an accusation against them as breakers of the law, he delivered them to be stoned."[14]

Many other early Jewish sources also refer to the existence of Jesus, and they confirm his existence as a historical fact. The Mishnah, together with ancient commentary on those teachings, form the Talmud, a famous collection of Jewish thought and literature. A reference to the death of Jesus is contained in the Sanhedren, one of the six orders or series under which the Mishnah is organized. The following words appear in the Sanhedren: "On the eve of Passover they hanged Yeshu (of Nazareth)."[15] Crucifixion in the first century was often referred to as "hanging on a tree" and that usage is found in the Dead Sea Scrolls, in the Mishnah itself, and in other Christian and non-Christian historical writings. It is clear, therefore, that historical references in non-Christian writings provide positive evidence of the actual existence of Jesus and of his crucifixion. Of course, numerous references to the historical existence of Jesus and his crucifixion exist in ancient contemporaneous, and substantially contemporaneous Christian writings.

Next, let us examine other independent and objective evidence to corroborate the many details set forth in the Gospel testimonies. In addition to the historical references described above, archaeological records, artifacts, medical opinions, and even astronomical observations provide ample substantiation for the testimony of the Gospels. We will begin at the beginning, with the story of the birth of Jesus in Bethlehem.

The Gospel of Matthew refers to an unusual star that hung over Bethlehem prior to the birth of Jesus (Matt. 2:2–11). The period during which Jesus is believed to have been born is between the year 7 B.C. and the year A.D. 7, with most scholars leaning toward 6 B.C. In 1603 John Kepler, a mathematician and astronomer, calculated that in either 6 or 7 B.C. the planets Jupiter and Saturn had moved so close to each other on the same degree of longitude that they had the appearance of a single, particularly brilliant large star. In fact, it has been determined that three such movements of the planets occurred during the year 7 B.C., in May, October, and in December, immediately before the year generally accepted as most likely for the birth of Jesus. Such an event is called a conjunction of the planets. In 1925 P. Schnabel, a German scholar, confirmed these events and the dates from translations of a Neo-Babylonian cuneiform found in the School of Astrology at Sippar, Babylonia. It is now believed that a conjunction of Saturn and Jupiter in the constellation Pisces must have occurred in 7 B.C.[16] An alternative source for the "Christmas Star," however, was proposed by three British astronomers recently. In 5 B.C., a supernova was observed for more than seventy days by Chinese astronomers of the Han Dynasty.[17] Either of these two unusual events would have been visible in the areas where the star was described in the Gospel of Matthew prior to the birth of Jesus.

The Gospel of Matthew also reported that Jesus was born in the town of Bethlehem, fulfilling a specific prophecy of the Old Testament prophet Micah, written seven hundred years before (Mic. 5:2). The ancient village was located on a ridge some six miles southwest of Jerusalem. In approximately A.D. 150, Justin Martyr wrote that Jesus was born in Bethlehem, and, "since Joseph could not find lodging in the village, he took up his quarters in a certain cave near the village; and while they were there Mary brought forth the Christ and placed him in a manger, and here the Magi who came from Arabia found him."[18] Caves often provided shelter for people and animals in the first century.

About one hundred years later, Origen wrote as if he had seen the cave himself, stating that "this sight is greatly talked of in surrounding places, even among the enemies of the faith, it being said that in this cave was born that Jesus who is worshiped and reverenced by the Christians."[19] Additional references to the cave, or grotto, and the special attention paid to it as the birthplace of Jesus are found in numerous other second-, third-, and fourth-century documents.

Today in Bethlehem, the sixth-century Church of the Nativity stands over the remains of a basilica, marking the location of an earlier church probably built by the emperor Constantine in A.D. 339. At the east end of the basilica is an altar which is directly above the same cave venerated from the first century as the "grotto of the nativity." This grotto is believed to mark the birthplace of Jesus.[20]

The Gospels report that Jesus grew up in the small town of Nazareth. Until recently, historians who were critical of the Bible suggested that Nazareth never existed. This was partially based upon the omission of any town by that name in listings of the main towns and villages of Galilee that were created by Josephus and that were listed by the Talmud. In the 1950s, however, the archaeologist Belarmino Begatti found silos, wells, granaries, millstones, an oven, a wine press, and olive and raisin presses in the exact location where Nazareth was believed to have been.[21] It was clearly an agricultural village. These artifacts date from the first century and were found beneath the present day town's Church of the Annunciation. We now have positive evidence that Nazareth existed as an agricultural community even before the time of Jesus. There is no reason to question the Gospel testimony that Jesus grew up there. This is bolstered by the description of the nature of Jesus in the Gospels of Luke and John discussed earlier.

The Church of the Annunciation in Nazareth was found to have been built above another church constructed in the twelfth century by Crusaders, and under it are the remains of an earlier Byzantine church. Within the outlines of the Crusader church is a small and deep rock cavern, a subterranean grotto. Eleventh-century writings describe the grotto as marking the place where Mary, the mother of Jesus, lived and was told that she was to bear the Messiah. It appears that the Crusader church was built to venerate the grotto. In A.D. 570, writings of Anonymous of Piacenza supported this traditional identification and reported that "the house of St. Mary is a basilica" located in Nazareth.[22] Nearby was found an ancient wine press believed to be from the Roman period, as well as an oven and grain silos.

In the early 1980s, Americans undertook an extensive excavation of the ancient city of Sepphoris, which traditionally is believed to be the birthplace of Mary. Located just three miles from Nazareth, Sepphoris is not mentioned in the Gospels, but it is mentioned in the Mishnaic references to Jesus described above. The city, according to Josephus, was the administrative capital of Galilee, symbolic of the new Roman culture. The discovery of Sepphoris shed new light on the early years of Jesus and the society in which he grew up. A cosmopolitan city connected by road to Nazareth, Sepphoris is mentioned by Josephus in his Jewish *Antiquities* for its prime strategic value to the Romans.

Excavations revealed a beautiful theater of marble capable of seating four thousand people, believed by archaeologists to have been built at the direction of Herod Antipas during the early part of the first century.[23] The Gospels refer to Jesus as a carpenter or a woodworker. Although this is speculation, it is reasonable to believe that artisans from Nazareth, possibly including Jesus, would have been employed in the building of this theater and other buildings in Sepphoris. Interestingly, it has been observed that Jesus used the word *hypocrite,* derived from Greek references to a play-actor, or a pretender, at least seventeen times in the Gospels. Scholars have therefore speculated that exposure to the culture of Sepphoris may have been responsible for this theatrical imagery.[24]

In any event, it is clear that the romanization of the area in the first century, as indicated by excavations in Sepphoris, would have had a great influence on the culture and economics of the entire area generally. Jesus and his followers were people who had been fully exposed to the sophistication of this city, and the demarcation between village life and city life was not as strong as had been believed. Three major roads ran near Nazareth, carrying pilgrims and Roman soldiers to Jerusalem as well as caravans moving between Egypt and Damascus.

In addition, the general understanding of Greek can be presumed from the influence of this romanized city. In particular,

Jesus' familiarity with Greek is supported by such details in the Gospels as the easy conversations between Jesus and a Roman centurion and with Pontius Pilate.[25] Moreover, the efficiency of the Roman postal system, discussed earlier, lends support to the current belief that society in this region, which could include Jesus and his disciples, was multilingual. It may also add to our understanding of the sophistication of the parables and metaphors used by Jesus in his teachings, notwithstanding his origins in the small town of Nazareth. Along with the new influence of the Roman culture, further evidence of the easy transport of manuscripts and letters undermines theories that the Gospel witnesses were necessarily ignorant provincials.

The Gospels report that as Jesus began his ministry, he was baptized by a person referred to as "John the Baptist." The baptism of Jesus at the beginning of his ministry is described in the various Gospels as occurring somewhere along the Jordan River. The Gospel of John also notes that one of the places in which John the Baptist performed his work was "Aenon near Salim, because there was plenty of water" (John 3:23 NIV). Professor W. F. Albright, an American archaeologist, has now identified Salim as being in the vicinity of Ainun.[26] The Gospels are clear that Jesus' baptism was somewhere other than Aenon, or Ainun, but this provides more circumstantial corroboration of the consistency of the details included in the Gospels.

Josephus confirmed Gospel testimony of the existence of "John, that was called the Baptist," describing him as a good and virtuous man who practiced baptism of the Jews in connection with the worship of God. He also confirmed the Gospel reports of the murder of John the Baptist by Herod at Machaerus, Herod Antipas's palace-fortress built near the Dead

Sea, and provided the names of Herodias, the wife of Herod, and her daughter, Salome.[27]

Many of the events described in the Gospels took place in Capernaum, near the Sea of Galilee. Until an excavation in 1866 the location of Capernaum was unknown, and many even doubted its existence. In that year Captain Charles Wilson, a British engineer, concluded that a site on the Sea of Galilee named Tel-Hum by local Arabs was in fact Capernaum.[28] Recent archaeological discoveries have now verified this identification.

In excavations carried on between 1905 and 1921, a second-to-fourth-century synagogue made of white limestone was discovered. In 1974, however, archaeologists found traces of a first-century synagogue made of four-foot-thick walls of black basalt, as well as the remains of residential sections. They also found pottery of the first decades of the first century in and under the floor. The excavator, Virgilio Corbo, concluded that we are now justified in believing that the first-century synagogue was the same synagogue referred to in the Gospel of Luke as having been built by a Roman centurion.[29] The Gospels of Matthew, John, and Luke all refer to Jesus' curing a servant of a Roman centurion in Capernaum (Matt. 8:5–13; Luke 7:2–10; John 4:46–53). The remains of a second- or third-century sixty-four-foot-long bathhouse of Roman design provide additional evidence of the Roman presence in Capernaum at that time. Beneath the bathhouse, archaeologists have found indications of a similar type of building from the first century.[30]

The importance of Capernaum to the early Christian community is indicated by the fact that the oldest Christian church uncovered by archaeologists has been located in the original site of that city. The church was built in a fashion that suggests that it commemorates a sacred place. It is in the form of an octagon, and coins and ceramics indicate that it was built in the fifth century. Nevertheless, records of a pilgrimage to the area in the early part of the fourth century described not only the church, but also include the following statement: "In Capernaum, moreover, out of the house of the first of the apostles a church has been made, the walls of which still stand just as they were. Here the Lord cured the paralytic."[31] In A.D. 570, the same church was described as a basilica that preserved the house of Peter.[32]

Archaeologists now believe that the house of Peter has been found beneath the remains of the octagonal church. The Gospels of Matthew and Mark both state that the apostles Simon Peter and Andrew owned a house in Capernaum and that Jesus spent much of the time during his last years in Capernaum. In fact, the Gospels of Matthew, Mark, and Luke all report that Jesus lived in Capernaum in the house of Peter and taught in the synagogue there (Matt. 8:14; Mark 1:29; Luke 4:38). Virgilio Corbo discovered in the lower levels of the excavated church the ruins of a house of the early first century. It appears to have been especially venerated over many centuries, having been constantly rebuilt with great attention.[33]

Graffiti written in many languages on fragments of plaster from the walls have been found. The writings particularly identify one of the rooms as a place with special meaning for early Christians. The words "Peter," "Christ have mercy," "Lord Jesus Christ help," and a Latin inscription with the names of Rome and Peter have all been found in these plaster fragments.[34] The graffiti also include many other symbols, such as a fish (which was used as a symbol of Christianity in the early church) and various crosses. Archaeologists have interpreted all of this to indicate that the house, and particularly the room described above, were especially venerated from the first century on, and that it was associated with, and perhaps was the home of, Peter.[35]

We have already discussed the finding of a fishing boat in Capernaum in recent years that is consistent with the descriptions in the Gospels of the fishing boat used not only by Peter, but also by Jesus and his disciples (Matt. 8:23; 9:1; 14:13; 15:39; Mark 4:36–38; 5:18, 21; 6:32, 45–51; 8:10, 14; Luke 5:1–11; 8:22–23, 37; John 6:16–25). The boat used by Jesus was generally described as being large enough to carry the disciples and capable of carrying a substantial cargo of fish.[36] The boat found at Capernaum fits that description.

Additionally, an unusual method of fishing described in the Gospels has been verified by modern fishing industry authorities in the Galilee region.[37] The Gospel of Luke describes two boats fishing together unsuccessfully all night. In the morning, at the command of Jesus who joined them, Peter let down the nets in deep water, and the sudden quantity of fish caught was so great that the nets began to break. Two boats working in tandem is traditional in Galilee when fishing for musht. Musht are generally caught at night and in a great mass at one time because they gather in shoals, exactly as described by Luke (see Luke 5:1–7). They are rarely caught singly.[38]

The Gospels describe many towns and miraculous events during Jesus' brief ministry. Almost every town mentioned in the Gospels has been identified by archaeologists today, providing more corroborative links in our chain of evidence. The Gospel of John reports that Lazarus was raised from the dead in the village of Bethany, and that this was one of the things that led to the demand for Jesus' death by Jewish authorities. John wrote that Jesus was in Bethany a few days before his death, and the Gospels of Matthew and Mark state that he lodged there at night during his final week in Jerusalem (Matt. 21:17–18; Mark 11:11–12; John 11).

The present village of el-'Azariyeh, located on the edge of the Mount of Olives approximately two miles from Jerusalem, has now been identified with the village of Bethany through historical references and archaeology. The ancient name "Lazarium," derived from Lazarus, developed into the present Arabic name. In approximately A.D. 330, Eusebius stated that the "place of Lazarus" was pointed out as Bethany, and in A.D. 390, Jerome noted that a church had been erected there to memorialize the tomb of Lazarus and the town.[39] In excavations conducted between 1949 and 1953, the Franciscans found numerous caves, tombs, and cisterns that revealed that this village had been inhabited from 1500 B.C. to approximately A.D. 100, and thereafter continuously from the sixth century to the fourteenth century. Clay lamps, earthen vessels, and coins from the time of Jesus were located in the excavations, including a coin of Herod the Great and one from the time of Pontius Pilate.

A tomb long venerated as that of Lazarus has been excavated in the location of Bethany. In A.D. 330, Eusebius referred to this tomb in a manner that suggested that it had been recognized as Lazarus's tomb for many years. It is in a cave dug from rocks, with a place for a large stone to cover it, all as reported in the Gospel of John (11:38).[40] From the entrance a visitor today steps down into a narrow passage leading five feet into a vaulted small inner chamber. On three sides of the chamber, niches appear in the wall for raised shelves to provide for three burials. Jerome, writing in A.D. 390, stated that a church had been built as a monument to this tomb, and the church was also noted by the pilgrim Aetheria who visited the village between A.D. 381 and 384.[41] Archaeologists believe the church mentioned in the fourth century was partially destroyed in an earthquake and was replaced around A.D. 427. Today a new Church of St. Lazarus stands on this site in the village of el-'Azariyeh in Israel.

The town of Magdala (or "Migdal," a variant of that name) is mentioned in the Gospels. It is believed that references to Mary Magdalene, a follower of Jesus, that occur in each of the Gospels mean "Mary, the one from Magdala" and that this was her home.[42] Magdala was in the location approximately where the small town of Migdal is today. Excavations conducted after 1971 show that Magdala was built according to Roman plan. Uncovered was a building believed to have been a synagogue from the period during which Jesus lived. The town also appears to have been the center of a fishing industry; one house contained a mosaic of a boat very similar to the fishing boat found in Capernaum in 1986. The house has been dated to the first century and was found approximately one mile from the location in the Sea of Galilee where the fishing boat described earlier was found.[43]

The Gospel of John, which covers a longer period of time for the ministry of Jesus than the other three, places Jesus in Jerusalem several times. All four Gospels relate that the last week of his life was spent in Jerusalem, however. As noted earlier, the Gospel of John makes many detailed and accurate references to geographical features of Jerusalem and its environs, evidencing personal familiarity with the city and its temple prior to destruction by the Romans in A.D. 70. For example, Jesus is described as healing a blind man and then telling him to "go, wash in the Pool of Siloam." The ancient pool of Siloam has been located in Jerusalem. It was excavated during 1896 and 1897 by archaeologists associated with the Palestine Exploration Fund. It is in the Tyropoeon Valley at one end of a tunnel, known as the Siloam Tunnel, which was built to provide a continuous source of water for Jerusalem in the event of an attack.

The pool has thirty-four steps, built of hard stones, with a portion cut from natural rock. The stairs were described by archaeologists as "well polished by footwear."[44] An inscription written on a stone slab indicates the original dedication of the Siloam Tunnel many hundreds of years before the birth of Jesus. The slab is now in a museum in Istanbul.[45] Of course, the pool was covered over by the destruction of Jerusalem in A.D. 70. A personal, immediate reference by an eyewitness to the pool's existence as given in the Gospel of John further corroborates that the author wrote prior to A.D. 70.

The temple in Jerusalem, prior to its destruction by the Romans, was the center of Jewish life. It was described with awe in the Gospels. Josephus wrote that it was covered with heavy plates of gold, which reflected a fiery splendor at the first rising of the sun. Some of the white limestone blocks with which it was built were enormous; at a distance, the temple appeared to strangers as a mountain of snow "for as to those parts of it that were not gilt, they were exceeding white."[46] Leen Ritmeyer, an American archaeologist, his wife Kathleen, an Irish archaeologist, and an English model-maker, Alec Garrard, have recently created a model reconstruction based upon archaeological findings and descriptions by contemporary eyewitnesses of the time that have been preserved.

Many of the large limestone blocks described by Josephus and also described in the Gospels have been found and are to be seen today,[47] as well as parts of the foundation structure, such as the original steps leading up to the southern entrance way.[48] Notices carved in stone warning Gentiles not to enter the inner courts upon pain of death have also been discovered. One found in the late nineteenth century and now at the Archaeological Museum in Istanbul is an almost complete version. The other is a partial construction found in 1935 and today held in Jerusalem's Rockefeller Museum.[49]

The Gospels report that the night before the crucifixion Jesus and his disciples went into a small estate, or garden, called Gethsemane (Matt. 26:36; Mark 14:32; John 18:1). The exact location of Gethsemane has not been determined, and two sites are currently preserved in Jerusalem by the Roman Catholic Church and the Greek Orthodox Church, respectively. In A.D. 330, Eusebius identified one site (now owned by the Roman Catholic Church) at the foot of the Mount of Olives as the place where Jesus prayed before his betrayal by Judas, reflecting long-standing local tradition.[50] Half a century later, in 381, the pilgrim Aetheria also reported in a journal that a church had been built to commemorate the second site as being the place where Jesus was betrayed.[51] The site marked by the Roman Catholic Church was excavated in 1909, and a large mass of rock was found immediately in front of the altar. Archaeologists believe, based partially upon a statement by Jerome in A.D. 390, that this was the rock mentioned in the Gospels, where Jesus prayed in Gethsemane.[52]

Recently Joan Taylor, a scholar from New Zealand, pointed out that the Aramaic and Hebrew translation of a word that is very similar to Gethsemane means "olive oil press," which in the first century was a large cave used for pressing olives into oil. Such a cave has now been located close to one of the two preserved gardens believed to mark Gethsemane. Historians have also found some evidence that this cave may have been the actual location referred to as Gethsemane in the Gospels.[53]

After Jesus was seized by soldiers in the Garden of Gethsemane, the Gospels report that he was first taken before the Pharisees and Caiaphas, the high priest who had planned his death. After the 1967 war in Jerusalem, the Israelis occupied Jerusalem's old Jewish Quarter and archaeologists began excavations. They uncovered several of the elegant villas owned by the priestly aristocracy near the location of the old temple mount. Twenty feet below the twentieth-century floor level a home now referred to as the Palatial Mansion was found. Overlooking the temple and the Lower City, the Mansion was originally two thousand square feet, two or three stories high, and built around a paved courtyard. Archaeologists believe that it may have belonged to the temple's high priest because of its baths and exquisite fresco decorations.[54] Additionally, archaeologists have speculated that this could be the house at which the apostle Peter waited at the time of Jesus' arrest as described in the Gospels.

Archaeologists believe that they have found the bones of Caiaphas, the high priest in Jerusalem between A.D. 18 and A.D. 37, reported by the Gospels to have presided over the trial of Jesus prior to his crucifixion.[55] Corroboration of this reference in the Gospel narrative is provided by Josephus, who specifically referred to this high priest twice, once as "Joseph Caiaphas," and thereafter, as "Joseph who was called Caiphas of the high priesthood."[56] In 1990 several Israeli workmen found a family tomb in an old cave south of the Old City of Jerusalem. Several limestone ossuaries, or depositories for bones, were found in the central chamber of the tomb. These have been dated around the time of Jesus. Ossuaries were not generally in use after A.D. 70 in Jerusalem. Inscriptions on one of the ossuaries bear the name "Joseph, son of Caiaphas," and contain the bones of four children, an adult woman, and a man of about sixty years old. It is believed that the bones of the sixty-year-old man are those of Caiaphas.[57]

Jesus was sent by Caiaphas to Pontius Pilate, the governor of Judea, to be tried and condemned to death. As we have seen, the occurrence and approximate date of the crucifixion of Jesus have been corroborated with historical evidence. The Roman historians Tacitus and Josephus both wrote that Jesus was executed during the reign of Pontius Pilate, while he was governor of Judea, confirming the Gospel accounts. Pontius Pilate's existence has been verified in other writings as well. Italian archaeologists in 1961 discovered in a Roman temple at Caesarea Maritima a stone inscription recording the dedication of a building commissioned by "Pontius Pilatus, Praefect of Judea to the Emperor Tiberius."[58] It has now been positively verified that Pontius Pilate was governor between A.D. 27 and A.D. 36, thus establishing a beginning and an end date for the period during which Jesus was crucified.

The Gospel of John also mentions a "Gabbatha," or pavement, where Pilate is said to have sat in judgment over Jesus prior to his crucifixion (John 19:13). L. H. Vincent, an archaeologist and priest, discovered this pavement,[59] which is preserved today in the crypt of the Covenant of the Sisters of our Lady of Zion in Jerusalem.[60]

Literary evidence of crucifixion in the first century as described in the Gospels is abundant. The Dead Sea Scrolls appear to refer to it as a punishment for treason, and it is known that the Romans used this as a means of execution for revolutionaries and thieves. From the beginning of the first century through A.D. 70 and the destruction of Jerusalem, thousands of people were crucified in Palestine. Two early crude graffiti of crucifixion have been found. One is from Pozzuoli, outside of Naples, the other from the Palatine Hill, near Rome.

In 1986, archaeological corroboration of the methods used for crucifixion was found by Israeli archaeologists. A skeleton of a first-century adult male who was crucified was found in an ossuary at an ancient Jewish cemetery in northern Jerusalem. An inscription on the ossuary identified the man by the name "Jehohanan." An iron spike was driven through the ankle bone, and a small piece of olive wood was still stuck to the spike.[61] The legs of the skeleton of Jehohanan were broken by a single, strong blow shortly before death precisely in the manner recorded in the Gospels for the thieves crucified beside Jesus (John 19:31–33).[62] Breaking the legs prevented the crucified person from raising himself in order to breathe and thus hastened his death, according to the custom of the times. This is believed to have been customary treatment for Jewish crucifixion victims in deference to the Mosaic prohibition against leaving the body on a cross after sundown at the beginning of the Sabbath.

Notwithstanding that custom, the Gospels report that the bones of Jesus were never broken—he was stabbed with a lance to assure his death. Critics, particularly German scholars, speculated decades ago that the story of the breaking of the legs was an invention of the Gospel writers, fabricated merely in order to fulfill an early prophecy in Psalm 34 that not one bone would be broken when the Messiah was crucified. Jehohanan's skeletal remains, however, undermine the theory of fabrication in the Gospels.

Medical opinions verify not only the Gospel report of the sweat of blood that Jesus suffered in Gethsemane the night before his crucifixion, but also the testimony in the Gospel of John that blood and water came out of the body of Jesus after he was pierced with a lance during the crucifixion (19:34, 35). Most medical experts agree that this is an accurate description of what would have been observed, since the water would have come from the pericardium surrounding the heart, and the blood from the right side of the heart. Some medical experts have observed that the water could also have been fluid accumulated in the lungs as a result of the beatings that Jesus suffered. All agree that this is strong proof of death.[63] In any event, it is unlikely that the apostle John could have known in the first century to fictionalize that effect.

The Turin Shroud is a length of linen that appears to bear imprints of a naked, crucified body. It is believed by some to be the very cloth purchased by Joseph of Arimathea to wrap the body of Jesus for burial, and if this is finally determined to be true, the shroud will provide stunning corroboration of many details of the Gospel testimony. This cloth was originally found in approximately A.D. 1350 in France. It appeared to bear marks made by blood and sweat, with outlines of a human face. Photographs of the shroud taken in 1898 and 1931 produced an astounding result; the photographic negatives showed a clear image of a man's face for the first time. The imprint shows swellings and blood on the face and encircling the forehead, as well as wounds near the hands at the location of the wrist and feet made by nails, and a wound on the right side of the chest, all exactly as described in the Gospel of John (John 19).[64] Both the front and the back of the cloth bear evidence of more than one hundred scourge marks on the body, made from a double-pronged whip with dumbbell-shaped balls of lead. The marks of the whip match the unique design of a Roman "flagrum" used in the first century.[65]

Scientists using carbon-14, or radiocarbon dating, at Oxford University and in two other laboratories in the United States and Switzerland tested small samples of the linen in 1988 and determined that the flax from which the shroud was woven "died" between A.D. 1260 and 1390. At the time, this appeared to be disappointing evidence that the shroud was a fake. Significant questions regarding the reliability of those test results have followed, however. Radiocarbon dating readings have now been determined to be influenced by atmospheric and environmental conditions, among other things, and recent anomalies have emerged concerning the accuracy of that method for woven materials.[66]

For example, in 1996, researchers from the University of Texas Health Science Center reported that radiocarbon dating was not reliable for the shroud because of a microscopic layer of bacteria and fungi on the linen that would be expected to affect dating for any ancient fabric.[67] This work of Dr. Leonicio Garza-Valdes has clearly shown that the linen is heavily contaminated with a mixture of bacteria and fungi and a clear, invisible bioplastic material which coats the fibers. The coating created by these microorganisms includes a high level of carbon-14 because of the presence of the bacteria and fungi, and this in turn would cause the fiber to be dated considerably later than the actual date of the cloth. What is not known today is the extent of the effect that the coating will have on the radiocarbon test date.[68]

It is also relevant that the shroud has been exposed to fire twice—once before the radiocarbon dating, at the palace of the House of Savoy in Chambery, France, in 1592, and again in April, 1997, when fire ravaged Turin Cathedral where it had been protected for four hundred years. In the 1592 fire, the shroud was scorched and then doused with water.[69] All living things, such as the original flax used to weave the shroud, contain carbon isotopes that decay after death. Radiocarbon dating measures the amount of carbon-14 that a former living thing contains. Dmitri Kouznetsov, a Russian biochemist, believes that the original 1988 analysis did not consider that exposure to fire would have increased the carbon atoms in the shroud, resulting in a later date for the artifact. While Kouznetsov's work is intriguing, it has not yet been confirmed by replication.[70] Although radiocarbon dating is still an extremely valuable tool, particularly for dating very early remains from the prehistoric period, it is not determinative, particularly with respect to ancient fabric, and many archaeologists have begun to search for "more controlled" ways to date their discoveries.[71]

Additionally, procedures used for the original testing have recently been challenged; some experts believe the test *methods* were unreliable and that new tests are required.[72] For example, the original protocol established by scientists in preparation for the testing in 1988 was abandoned with no public explanation. The protocol required that six samples from the linen shroud would be provided for testing by seven different laboratories. In the end, only one sample was provided and it was divided into three pieces, to be tested by three laboratories. Additionally, although correct procedure is to require representative and homogeneous samples that reflect the condition of the whole cloth, the sample that was provided was taken from only one corner of the shroud. A recent comparison of the shroud sample to another area of the cloth, using infrared microspectrophotometry and a scanning electron microprobe, revealed differences in chemical composition between the two areas.[73]

Further clouding the assignment of the radiocarbon test date, circumstantial evidence traces the shroud as far back as the first century. For example, art from a period prior to the radiocarbon test date appears to show the shroud; and two professors of computer science and forensic medicine, respectively, say that they have identified a faint image of a Roman coin from A.D. 29 on the cloth.[74] References believed to be to the shroud have been found in historical writings as early as the first century, in the city of Edessa, in Turkey. This cloth was referred to as the "image of Edessa," in Edward Gibbon's history *The Decline and Fall of the Roman Empire*.[75]

Lovely spring flowers provide evidence that the origin of the shroud was the geographic area around Jerusalem, and, if the shroud is authentic, support the testimony of the Gospels that Jesus was crucified in spring, at the time of the Feast of Passover. Pollen grains of plants and faint images of plants, especially sprinkled around the head, were discovered on the shroud. In 1973, Max Frei, a forensic scientist from

Switzerland, identified fifty-eight species of plants among hundreds of pollen grains taken from the linen.[76] The pollen has also been found to match many species that are peculiar to the environs of Jerusalem.

In 1997, it was announced that twenty-eight different specimens of plants had been identified through images that appear on the shroud under a special process of photography, using negatives and ultraviolet light scanning to increase the contrast. Botanists from Hebrew University have authoritatively matched these images to plants, some of which grow only in the area between Jerusalem and Jericho. The plants include rock roses, crown chrysanthemums, and a bouquet of bean capers. The bean caper grows only in Israel, Jordan, and the Sinai desert, and the faint images on the shroud of the winter leaves and the stalks indicate that the plant was picked in the spring, the time of the crucifixion as reported in the Gospels.[77]

The jury should also consider that the pollen and the plant images establish a presence in Palestine not reflected in historical records of the shroud since its discovery in A.D. 1350, suggesting an earlier date for those travels. Numerous well-respected artists have attempted to reproduce the image on the shroud without success; they are unable to convert a model of the human face to a negative image. The image has been determined from computer analysis to be three dimensional, and it cannot be reproduced. The features of the face are not symmetrical, as one would expect, and that is a dissimilarity that has not been evidenced in the work of any artist from the Middle Ages or earlier. Of course, the technique of photography and the concept of negative images were unknown in the thirteenth or fourteenth centuries.[78]

The shroud's image of a body and apparent bloodstains are extremely convincing, so much so that today many well-respected specialists, including medical experts, have concluded that it is an actual cloth that was wrapped around someone who was crucified in a manner identical to that reported for Jesus in the Gospels, regardless of its date. Samples from the marks indicating blood on the image of the face and body have been subjected to chemical analysis and have been determined to be exuded blood. The particles are hemoglobin, type AB.[79] Blood does not flow from a dead person, however. These blood stains appear to have been created by contact of moist blood clots with clear borders of serum lines, not from a fresh flow of blood. When photographed, the serum lines, which can only form around blood clots, produce fluorescent halos around the blood marks, indicating that these were from the last blood that flowed near death and at the time of death.[80]

In 1995 earlier samples taken from the bloodstains on the shroud tested positive for DNA (believed to be of human source) in research performed by Marcello Canale at the Institute of Legal Medicine in Genoa, Italy. Three gene segments have been clearly isolated. These results were subsequently verified by Victor and Nancy Tryon at the Center for Advanced DNA Technologies. Additionally, in the second analysis the presence of X and Y male chromosomes were confirmed.[81]

Neither the image nor the bloodstains on the shroud were created with paint; this has been confirmed with micrographs taken in 1978 at sixty-four times magnification and also by detailed chemical analysis.[82] Extensive testing showed that there is no paint medium coating the fibers, and no stains or dyes caused it. The discoloration of the fibers in the image has been established to be the result of a degradation of the fibers, a chemical change that is not understood.[83] While the blood stains appear to have been created by a contact process, the image was not created in this way. Experiments with various processes whereby a comparable linen cloth was placed in direct contact with the front and sides of a subject's face as required for a three-dimensional image resulted in a flat, distorted, or spread-out picture. The process of formation of the image remains unknown.[84]

The radiocarbon dating results are thus inconsistent with the rest of the scientific data currently available on the shroud. Because of this circumstantial evidence, even in the face of radiocarbon dating, many experts now question the proposition that the shroud is a forgery.[85] Although questions remain unanswered, the jury is entitled to consider and weigh the value of the shroud as evidence that corroborates the Gospel descriptions of the crucifixion and burial of Jesus, and perhaps even indirectly the resurrection itself.

The Gospels report that, after his death, the body of Jesus was given to a friend, Joseph of Arimathea, to be placed in Joseph's private tomb. Roman law as recorded in the ancient Digest of Justinian verifies that the bodies of executed persons at that time were required to be given to anyone who requested them for burial.[86]

Corroborating evidence regarding the description in the Gospels of the tomb in which Jesus was buried is impressive. More than sixty examples of similar tombs used at the time Jesus lived, with large rolling-stone boulders that seal the entrance, just as described in the Gospels, have been found in and around Jerusalem.[87] Two sites have been identified as possibly being the site of Jesus' tomb; both are located in Jerusalem. The most likely site was described in the early third century by Eusebius and in writings of a pilgrim known as the Bordeaux Pilgrim. It was located near the hill of Golgotha, referred to by the Gospels of Mark, Matthew, and John as "the Place of a Skull" (Matt. 27:33; Mark 15:22; John 19:17).[88] The favored location was marked by a "church of wonderful beauty" built by Constantine, the first Christian emperor of the Roman Empire. On this site today is the Church of the Holy Sepulcher, which was built at the time of the Crusades. Within the church is a small building that contains a marble slab, covering what has been traditionally accepted as the actual site of the tomb of Jesus.[89]

That tradition has been based primarily upon the following information. As recorded by several fourth-century historians, at the site when first shown to Helena, the mother of emperor Constantine, stood a temple dedicated to Aphrodite. Helena removed the temple and beneath found three crosses in a tomb. Within the tomb was found a *titulum* stating that the person crucified was the "King of the Jews," written in Aramaic, Greek, and Latin, exactly as reported in the Gospel of John. The *titulum* is on display in the Basilica of Santa Croce in Rome, though its authenticity has not been established beyond all question.[90] Early historical references tend to support this story. In A.D. 348, shortly before Easter, Cyril of Jerusalem delivered a series of lectures in a building that preceded the Church of the Holy Sepulcher. In these lectures Cyril made reference to the discovery of the cross on which Jesus was crucified. Additionally, several fourth-, fifth-, and sixth-century historians made mention of three crosses claimed to have been found in this location.[91]

Because the spot discovered by Helena was especially marked at such an early time, it is believed that there is a reasonable case for accepting the location of the Church of the Holy Sepulcher as the genuine site of the tomb in which Jesus was buried.[92] This is bolstered by the apparent tenacity with which Helena excavated this particular site. According to the testimony of the Gospels, the tomb was originally located outside of the walls surrounding Jerusalem. At the time Helena began her search, however, the walls had been rebuilt and the location was actually inside the new walls. Because Helena was not deterred by this historical discrepancy, it has been suggested that there must have been some compelling evidence causing Helena to ignore the apparent conflict with the Gospel description.[93]

Archaeologist Kathleen Kenyon discovered in 1960 that the wall had been moved outward from its original location prior to the time of Helena's arrival. The Church of the Holy Sepulcher is now known to be located on a site that was in fact originally outside of the city walls as they stood at the time that Jesus lived, consistent with the Gospel testimony. Not much of the tomb is left today because of repeated Muslim attacks on the city over the centuries, as well as the extensive excavation by Constantine's engineers at Helena's direction.[94] The previously mentioned lectures of Cyril of Jerusalem in A.D. 348 also described the location of the tomb as a garden, confirming the testimony of the Gospel of John that Jesus was buried in a new tomb in a garden.[95]

The evidence offered to the jury verifies the reliability of the statements made by our witnesses regarding the details and framework within which their testimony rests. But direct evidence of the resurrection is provided by the eyewitness testimony of Matthew, Mark, and John, as corroborated by Luke, and the credibility of each of these witnesses has been further corroborated by all of the documentary, archaeological, and scientific evidence presented above. Focusing our case merely upon the resurrection of Jesus as reported in the Gospels, we have seen that each witness stated as a simple fact that the resurrection occurred in bodily form. It is significant that this particular testimony is given independently and very explicitly by all four witnesses. It is clear that each witness understood what was being said about this fact, and the testimonies recite the resurrection as an event that was actually observed as reality, not as mythology or metaphor or tradition.

In that regard, the belief of others in the community in the fact of the resurrection is also corroborative. They act to ratify the statements in the Gospels that the resurrection occurred. The letters of Peter, Paul, and James in books of the New Testament other than the Gospels, as well as the Book of Acts, written by Luke, and the works of other authors described throughout this chapter, are therefore presented as corroborative links in the chain of evidence in our analysis, under the same authentication procedures that were set forth in the beginning of this case, as required by the Federal Rules of Evidence for an ancient document. These other books of the New Testament, and the writings of other authors contemporaneously and after the time that the Gospels began to be circulated, clearly indicate that the belief in the community, of the people who actually knew the authors and those in the Christian community immediately thereafter, was that the crucifixion and resurrection of Jesus had in fact occurred.

The conviction of Paul in the truth of the resurrection is set forth in his own signed letters contained in the New Testament, and this conviction appears to have crystallized at the time of his conversion as early as A.D. 33, almost immediately after the crucifixion.[96] Many of these letters were written to various early churches before and during a period known as his second mission; the date for this mission has been established by reference in the Book of Acts to the description of Paul's appearance before the Achaean proconsul Gallio during that period. Archaeologists have confirmed the fact that Gallio's administration has been accurately dated up to A.D. 51 or 52 at the latest, by an inscription found at Delphi.[97] Ten of the letters from Paul contained in the New Testament are assigned dates between A.D. 48 and 68.[98] The letters reflect that Paul held his belief in the resurrection of Jesus from the moment of his conversion about A.D. 33 to such an extent that he was willing to die for that conviction at that time.[99]

A letter mentioned earlier from Paul to the Corinthians, dated A.D. 54 to 56 by various sources, contains a statement by Paul that more than five hundred people witnessed the resurrected Jesus, and that many of those witnesses were still alive at the time of the writing of this letter. The authenticity of this letter has never been seriously challenged.[100] In this same letter Paul clearly acknowledged that if Christ had not been raised from the dead, then all of the preaching of his followers and the faith of the early Christians would be in vain (see 1 Cor. 15:12–21).

The reliability of the letters of Paul as evidence are supported by the fact that many details in those letters have also been verified.[101] For example, Paul referred to a city treasurer named Erastus, in his Epistle to the Romans, which he wrote from Corinth. During excavations of Corinth in 1929, a pavement was found with the inscription "Erastus, curator of public buildings, laid this pavement at his own expense."[102] Other letters of Paul and of Peter and James containing references to the resurrection are also believed to have been written at very early dates.

All of the evidence that has been presented to the jury in this case must be sifted and weighed to determine its *cumulative* effect. Now let us turn to the final argument—the summation of the facts and the evidence, and the application of the law to the evidence. The purpose is to assist you in your analysis and evaluation of the evidence, but it is also meant to persuade. This is the summary of the case for the truth of the testimony of the witnesses, Matthew, Mark, Luke, and John. Here we are permitted to begin to draw legitimate inferences from the evidence.

CHAPTER SEVEN

Summation to the Jury

LADIES AND GENTLEMEN OF THE JURY:

T wo thousand years ago a man of unremarkable appearance was nailed to a cross. He was born in a cave and grew up in a small village like a tender shoot, like a root out of parched ground. He had no stately form or majesty when looked upon, no appearance that would attract others to him. In the entire New Testament not one reference to his appearance is given. In fact, he was despised and forsaken, a man of sorrows and acquainted with grief. He was crucified with thieves, yet he was buried in the tomb of a rich man. He poured out himself to death, yet he interceded for the ones who had condemned him. This was his life and this was his death—and the words were written by the prophet Isaiah some 740 years before the events occurred. The words have been preserved in scrolls dated to hundreds of years before the birth of this man.

And then on the third day after death and burial, this man returned to life, fully and completely, to walk among his friends, family, and followers and to speak with them. This too was foretold before it occurred—by Isaiah and others in the Old Testament, and even by this man, precisely and clearly. Translated into our language, this man's name was Jesus.

These events were described by four witnesses in plain and simple language. The testimony, preserved in books we call the Gospels, is written without artifice or embellishment, but is given in great detail. The story as it is told by each of the witnesses is placed within a historical framework referencing dates, people, places, and surrounding events—all facts that can, and have been, verified. The witnesses who gave the testimony were just plain and simple men whose lives reflected honor and goodness consistently.

The evidence has shown that our witnesses had no motive or incentive to fabricate the testimony. On the contrary, in the first century the penalty for belief in the truthfulness of the gospel message was too great to provide any rational basis to assume otherwise. The personal sacrifice that necessarily accompanied this belief also diminishes any argument that the witnesses would have been inclined to falsely teach the word to others who would suffer as a result. Such falsehood is inconsistent with their lives and conduct as it is known historically. Additionally, evidence has been presented to clearly establish the absolute conviction of these witnesses that the resurrection of Jesus actually occurred.

The character—that is, the personal courage and honor of these witnesses—including Luke, the investigator—has been shown by the results of their lives. We have seen that anyone who taught the word of the gospel or lived it at that time, including the authors, had to be a person of great courage and moral character, willing to die for principle. People do not die for what they *know* to be false. The only logical inference consistent with the conduct of the witnesses is that our four witnesses were people of honor. The initial presumption under the law of honesty and capability of the witnesses has been confirmed by corroboration of the details of the testimony. The integrity of the character of the witnesses has been established.

The jury has also been presented with evidence that the people who received the Gospels from our witnesses believed them to be honorable. The community provided an independent monitor of accuracy and truthfulness. Moreover, we know that the communities in which these Gospels were written placed a very high premium on accuracy. If the Gospels had been inaccurate or false, they would not have been so widely accepted without criticism. In contrast, the community's lack of criticism and acceptance of the teachings is evidenced by conduct consistent with those teachings.

We have emphasized the importance of the intensity of the belief that each person in the community seemed to hold in the truthfulness of the testimony of the four witnesses. The conduct of that group of people, as well as the conduct of Matthew, Mark, Luke, and John, has been presented to the jury as evidence of ratification of the accuracy and truth of the Gospel testimony as to the fact of the resurrection of Jesus. Those who have attempted to discredit the state of mind of these witnesses have argued that their conduct was based upon psychological manipulation, and possibly hallucinations. The weakness of that position is revealed when the jury considers that these events of martyrdom did not occur all at one time in one place, as would be required to support a claim that they were based upon mass hysteria or collective reaction to manipulative suggestion by a charismatic leader. Rather, they occurred in a consistent and sustained pattern through the lifetimes of these witnesses and their successors, over twenty, thirty, and forty years, in diverse geographical locations, often with no other follower participating.

Moreover, this conduct was not the result of passive compliance that underlies most psychological manipulation. The jury has seen that, in many cases of Christian martyrdom, escape from the ultimate penalty would have been available through repudiation, and yet it was strength of character that upheld principle even to death. As we have seen from evidence presented to the jury, this fact is historically evident in the writings of Pliny (the Younger), who saw the refusal of followers of Jesus to repudiate their beliefs as stubbornness and unshakeable obstinacy when freedom was offered in return; or in the terrible death of Ignatius, who was given many chances to disavow his belief prior to being sent to the arena. The emperor Trajan advised that a person denounced as a Christian was to be punished, but "if any one denies that he is a Christian, and actually proves it, that is by worshipping our gods, he shall be pardoned as a result of his recantation, however suspect he may have been with respect to the past."[1] This refusal to disavow belief in the teachings of the gospel shows strength of character reflecting firm belief, not passive compliance. That belief, evidenced by conduct, provides us today with an opinion of those in the communities of Matthew, Mark, Luke, and John that the testimony of these four witnesses is truthful.

The "hallucination" argument is defeated for the same reasons. The Gospel testimony is that many people saw Jesus after the resurrection in different places and at different times. It is impossible to believe that they all experienced the same hallucinations because hallucinations are subjective and personal to the subject making the claim. "By their very nature, only one person can see a given hallucination at a time."[2]

The credibility of the Gospels is further supported by evidence presented to the jury that our witnesses were all of the generation born during the time that Jesus lived and the events occurred. Historical evidence has been presented to show that all of the Gospels were written prior to A.D. 70 when Jerusalem was destroyed, and probably much earlier. In addition, by matching the earliest manuscripts to papyrus fragments from even earlier manuscripts, you have seen that the Gospels of Matthew, Mark, and Luke can be dated within approximately thirty-three to thirty-six years of the death of Jesus at the very latest, and they were already circulated throughout a wide portion of the Roman Empire at those dates. The original manuscripts were, of course, written even earlier. In fact, evidence of the certainty of an earlier manuscript of the Gospel of Matthew appears in ancient references to such a Gospel written in Aramaic, prior to the earliest Greek fragments that have been preserved.

The early dating of the manuscripts of the Gospels permits us to infer reasonably that the testimony of Matthew, Mark, and John reflects firsthand observation by these witnesses. The Gospels are written from the perspective of firsthand observers, and there is no reason to disbelieve that these people were eyewitnesses of the events reported. Some portions of Luke also reflect firsthand observation, although that Gospel has been presented to the jury primarily as a carefully conducted investigation of events that were publicly known.

Although history and logic provide evidence to support personal attribution of each Gospel to a particular individual, the jury should also recognize that personal attribution is not necessary to establish either the firsthand nature of the testimony, or the integrity of that testimony. We have seen that *whoever* these authors were, they lived within the generation span of Jesus and thus had the opportunity to observe the events. That they did in fact observe those events is established not only by the great precision and detail of their descriptions, but also by external corroborating evidence that the details are correct. These details of the fundamental points of the testimony and the historical framework of the narratives have been shown to be consistent among the witnesses in material part.

Verifiable evidence of the historical fact of the life and crucifixion of Jesus has been presented to the jury. Looking back over the horizon of history, you have seen that references to his life were preserved in writings of many non-Christian historians from the period beginning immediately after his death and throughout the following centuries, including Tacitus, Suetonius, Josephus, Pliny (the Younger), Trajan, and Thallus, and in the Talmud, well-known early Jewish literature. Further proof is supplied by numerous Christian writers of the period and by extensive archaeological evidence and other evidence that corroborates the fact of his existence and the manner of his death. In fact, the evidence that has been presented to the jury corroborates almost every single detail by which the historical and social context of the testimony has been created.

But it is the claim of resurrection that provides the greatest authentication to the special nature of Jesus. That claim is based upon the actual testimony of the Gospel witnesses. We have seen that federal law holds that direct eyewitness testimony is powerful evidence not to be easily disregarded. The inference of truth of the facts to be proved by that testimony depends upon the truthfulness, or credibility, of the witness.[3] The witnesses, Matthew, Mark, Luke, and John, have testified through the Gospels that they and hundreds of others observed the crucifixion and the resurrection, that they saw and spoke with Jesus at this time, that he appeared in recognizable form after death, and that their relationships with him continued after his physical death.

Evidence of the truthfulness, or credibility, of the witnesses has been presented to the jury. In addition, evidence has shown that the testimony of the four Gospels regarding the resurrection are all harmonious, original, and prepared without concert. Discrepancies among the four Gospels do not create material inconsistencies among them. But they show imperfections of memory that are believable and to be expected in testimony from people who observed the same event from different perspectives.

The corroborative evidence presented to the jury as proof of the reliability and credibility of the testimony of the Gospel witnesses may be relied upon with the same weight that would be attributed to other sources of authority. If you are planning to take a trip, you may call a travel agent or look at a map; if you are looking for information about China, you may rely upon an encyclopedia, or you may turn to video information. It is common in the world of science to base research upon predicates established in literature published by authorities in the discipline. The same is true for knowledge based upon history. The reliability of the contents of the information accepted as true may be weighed or tested against your personal knowledge or against other authorities, but the method of receiving and accepting information based upon an authoritative source is acceptable scholarly protocol.

It is true that testimony of a fact that is not explained by our current understanding of the laws of nature is difficult for us to accept because we cannot comprehend how it happened. Science has no explanation for the resurrection of Jesus of Nazareth even today. We have seen that failure to understand the cause of an event is not a reason to reject solid evidence that the event occurred, however. That is a very fundamental point upon which all scientific research is based. The fact that we cannot understand something does not mean that it is contradictory to the laws of nature. Science, which has been described as the gatekeeper to reason and truth, has adopted the protocol that credible evidence must never be rejected merely because it is not understood.

If we were to be limited only to what we know and can verify from personal experience, human knowledge would stagnate. That is why the law, and science, permit us to reason and infer facts from circumstances. The fact that we cannot understand the resurrection of Jesus does not diminish the value of the evidence that has been presented to you, the jury. Science has no explanation for many things that exist in our physical world today, yet we continue to try to understand the consequences of things even when we cannot explain the cause.

For those who remain skeptical because of the fact that we cannot understand as a matter of science how these things could have occurred, recall that science is not yet even close to explaining how human life began. After many years of concentrated efforts, "origin of life" science has no answers. The improbability involved in generating even the simplest form of life is so enormous that the famous British astronomer Sir Frederick Hoyle compared it to the chance that "a tornado sweeping through a junk-yard might assemble a Boeing 747 from the materials therein."[4] If we cannot even understand our own existence, how can we dismiss other events asserted as factual merely because we cannot understand their cause? Our own lives are unexplained, yet we know that we exist!

The underlying premise of the resurrection, that God exists and life after death is possible, is also not inconsistent with our current scientific understanding of the universe and living organisms. You have seen that the Big Bang model of the universe requires a first cause that is not governed by our natural laws and that is not understood from a scientific perspective. Science has also provided overwhelming evidence that the universe and living organisms within the universe were intelligently designed. This is shown by evidence on a cosmic level that such things as the formation of the galaxies and the creation of heavy elements and light elements occurred at exactly the right time and in exactly the right ratio, or balance, to permit life to occur. The rational inference is that the first cause of the universe was not just a creative force but an intelligent creator.

The jury may be concerned about an obvious problem: At first glance an argument for design that relies upon the delicate balance of the physical aspects of the universe may appear vulnerable to an argument that things could appear to be the result of design merely because we are able to view them after the fact. In other words, perhaps all of these things occurred randomly and by chance, but even that hypothesis is destroyed by the new understanding that we have now developed about such things as biochemical microsystems.

Michael Behe, a biochemist who wrote an excellent book describing these biochemical microsystems, analogized the problem to a Rube Goldberg contraption you may remember from childhood cartoons.[5] Like biological microsystems, the Rube Goldberg machine was irreducibly complex, a single system composed of many parts that interact to contribute to the basic function. The removal of any one of the parts caused the system to cease functioning. The Rube Goldberg machine began with a dollar bill acting as bait for Foghorn Leghorn. The dollar bill was attached to a string on a stick. The stick propped up a ball. When the bait was taken and the bill was moved, the stick moved and the ball rolled off a cliff, hitting the raised end of a seesaw. On the other end of the seesaw was a rock with sandpaper attached to it. The rock flew up, igniting a flame by striking a match on its upward journey. The flare lit the fuse to a cannon, and the cannon fired a cannonball that hit a lever that started a circular saw. The saw cut through a rope holding up a telephone pole, and the pole fell—on Foghorn Leghorn. This is an irreducibly complex system. Every component of the system depends upon efficient performance by every other part.

The human blood-clotting system is also an irreducibly complex microsystem. The absence of any one of a number of its components, as in the Rube Goldberg machine, will cause the system to fail. Each component of the system activates another, and the timing is crucial. Many such irreducibly complex biochemical systems exist in our bodies. Random development of systems like these by numerous, successive, slight modifications would not work, because without *all* of the elements of the system being in place *from the beginning* the system will not be able to function. The elements are interdependent. In fact, in the case of the blood-clotting system, by analogy, if the first few steps required for operation of the system were in place without the last few steps being in place, the human organism would bleed to death with the first superficial wound.[6]

It is also important to consider that not one piece of scientific literature has ever been published to explain in detail, step by step, how an irreducibly complex biochemical system could have evolved through random selection, in any manner. Even those who have argued hypothetically that the system may have evolved through genetic mutations are unable to explain the details of such an evolutionary process or, more important, the origin of such a hypothetical genetic map. Behe has concluded that since there is no gradual route to the production of these complex microsystems, a design is evident.[7]

Evidence that consciousness and personal identity can transcend physical limitations, as implied by the resurrection, is also consistent with current scientific understanding, or lack of understanding. Neither neurologists, neurophysicists, nor philosophers have been able to explain how "consciousness" occurs in the human thought process. An understanding of human consciousness remains one of the greatest mysteries of science, but it is almost universally accepted that it cannot be explained in physical terms today.[8] Without such an explanation, we are left with a premise that our minds are something separate from the physical, and we are therefore more than the sum of our physical parts.

This conclusion is also consistent with the findings of researchers on near-death experiences, some of which have been empirically verified. Medical and other neuroscientific experts report that studies performed on claims of subjects who were physically unconscious and declared medically dead (prior to resuscitation) find that those subjects were able to observe, report, and later remember certain facts that cannot be explained by our own knowledge of the workings of the brain. Many thousands of people have reported this experience. In a few cases it has been objectively established by medical verification that these subjects reported facts or events that it was not possible for them to know or observe from the physical position in which they were placed at the time; in other words, they saw and reported things that it was physically impossible for them to know or see. The accuracy of the observations have been carefully checked against medical records of the subjects, together with other evidence. No satisfactory medical or scientific explanation has been established for these reports, and standard speculations as to physical causes, such as an overabundance of carbon dioxide in the brain or hypoxia, or the rapid destruction of cells on the perimeter of the brain, have been convincingly rebutted.[9]

These cases suggest that some element of the human organism has separated from the physical body to accomplish an experience that occurs outside of the body. This also implies the existence of a mind that is separate from the brain, something extra and non-physical, and not as yet completely understood. Philosophers and theologians could call this a soul. We do not yet understand these events, and we do not understand the reappearance of Jesus after his death. But, it is fair to say that the continuation of personal identity of Jesus after his death, like the unknown element of human consciousness which seems to transcend physical limitations, is not a fact that is contradicted by current scientific knowledge.

We have examined the credibility of the witnesses, Matthew, Mark, Luke, and John, and the corroborating evidence for their testimony that Jesus lived, died, and returned to life. The existence and crucifixion of Jesus have been proven with empirical evidence as well as through the testimony of the witnesses. Evidence of the resurrection is based upon testimony of credible witnesses. As to the resurrection, if we can accept as facts such events as the creation of the universe, black holes, quantum particles, the origin of life, the evolution of subcellular biochemical systems in the human body, and human consciousness without understanding the cause, then we cannot reject testimony of credible, truthful witnesses on the basis that we do not understand the cause of the reported occurrence.

In spite of all of this evidence, however, many intelligent people who have taken the time to study the origin of the four Gospels appear to have surrendered their objectivity to a desire to confirm the hypothesis that the Gospels are merely stories built upon myth and legend.

Because the Gospels are consistent in the telling, these individuals have assumed that the common cause of this consistency was that the Gospels were written in concert. They failed to acknowledge the straightforward explanations for the commonality of the Gospels that have been presented to the jury today—that is, that witnesses repeating the observation of the same set of facts, even when given from different perspectives, will be expected to be consistent in material respects. We have also seen that this principle is bolstered by the use of shorthand and memorization before, during, and after the first century, the seriousness with which the duty of transmission of information was held, and differences resulting from modern translations of the early texts.

Because the Gospels represent the consistent belief of the early Christian community, as evidenced by the historical fact of conduct in the face of persecution, these critics have assumed that the Gospels were written after the stories were developed and the conduct occurred, merely to *memorialize* the beliefs and stories and conduct. They assumed that the myths and legends were the cause of the conduct and writings, rather than understanding that the writings merely reflected the truth upon which the conduct was based. This is a confusion of cause and effect; it is a common fallacy in logical reasoning when the two things, cause and effect, occur at almost the same time. But this ignores the evidence presented by the papyrus fragments and all of the other evidence that has been presented to you, the jury, that prove that the entire Gospels were written at a date early enough to indicate eyewitness observation and too early for the full development of myths and legends regarding the events.

You have also seen evidence that the Gospels were written at a time when hundreds of other people in the community who had also observed these events were still alive to act as monitors of the truth and accuracy of the testimony. These "myths and legends" theories ignore all of the verifiable evidence available today that the full manuscripts were in place almost contemporaneously with the events reported. The evidence is the key, however; it effectively destroys any proposition that the Gospels were developed over hundreds of years, or even generations, of mere tradition.

The jury may ask why these theories have been popularly adopted, and the answer may be as simple as human frailty. When intellectual analysis becomes more interesting than simple truth, that analysis will be developed. And as years pass, each person who has invested time and a career in the development of the hypothesis finds that it is more difficult to become objective: the vested interest must now be protected. This may not necessarily involve a conscious decision; the fallacy of rejecting negative evidence is born of human nature. Evidence that tends to disprove a case becomes bad news.

And because the "myths and legends" hypothesis must be supported, there developed endless analyses as to why each witness said what was said in each Gospel. For example, questions as to such things as the nature of the character of Jesus, as presented by the testimony of the Gospels, caused a search not for evidence of the truth of the statements but rather a search for the tradition by which the testimony was influenced. The query became what political goal was sought to be achieved by the author of the corresponding Gospel. The motivation behind each statement rather than the truth of the statement became the subject for inquiry. Evidence that did not support the "myths and legends" hypothesis was rejected or overlooked. The cart was put before the horse; result-oriented assumptions were proposed upon which analyses were based in order to come to a predetermined conclusion—and the simple facts as told in the four Gospels became twisted and obscured.

It is very important to separate fact from theory in a search for truth. When a jury is asked to weigh the evidence, it is being asked to sort through all of the information that has been presented to it and to determine how convincing the evidence is and whether it will support the conclusion that has been proposed. In evaluating the testimony, recall that almost every event surrounding the fundamental testimony of the Gospels has been verified today by archaeology and other sciences. The jury has been presented with evidence both direct and circumstantial to prove the facts at issue. In each aspect of the case you have received information to support each conclusion; no assumptions have been made without a rational foundation of proof; no blind faith has been required.

In many cases, evidence found within the past few decades has even given credence to facts that have previously been considered suspect. Almost every town, most of the locations within a town or territory, and every governmental or local ruler or authority mentioned in the Gospels have now been proven to have existed and been in place at the reported time. The cumulative impact of the verification of almost every detail of the Gospels by independent evidence is important because it is so difficult for a false witness to maintain consistency in his or her own testimony. That is particularly true with testimony of four different witnesses to the same events. For that reason, variety and scope of detail are excellent predictors of truth.

You are now asked to determine whether the truth of the testimony of the Gospels is supported by a preponderance of the evidence, the standard of proof required in a civil trial in a federal court in the United States of America. Does the evidence that has been offered to you in this case permit you to find that the testimony of the Gospels that Jesus lived two thousand years ago and died on the cross and returned to life is more likely than not to be so? It is here submitted that the evidence presented to the jury in this case provides an abundance of proof upon which to base a verdict that the Gospels are true.

Once evidence has been presented that is sufficient for a reasonable person to infer that the facts alleged are more likely than not to be true, the burden of going forward to offer evidence and persuade the jury to the contrary shifts to the adversary for all practical purposes. In fact, direct evidence—that is, eyewitness testimony such as that of Matthew, Mark, and John—in the absence of extremely convincing contrary proof would *require* the court to instruct the jury that the truth of the facts supported by this evidence is the only rational inference.[10] In either case, the adversary who claims that these events did not occur would be required to present sufficient proof to *outweigh* a reasonable inference from the positive evidence that the facts did occur. In two thousand years, that has never been done with regard to the life, death, and resurrection of Jesus.

The burden of producing evidence is usually upon
the party who has pleaded the existence of the fact.
The burden may shift to the adversary when the
pleader has discharged its initial duty however.[11]

This burden has not been met by those who claim that the Gospels are mere myth and legend. When determining the weight to give to the testimony of witnesses such as Matthew, Mark, Luke, and John, instructions to a jury that have been approved in federal court ask the jury to decide whether there was evidence to prove the witnesses testified falsely concerning some important fact, or whether other evidence offered in the case was inconsistent with the testimony of the witnesses.[12] The testimony of the Gospels has not yet been subjected to verifiable controverting evidence of that quality by critics.

The jury should consider the fact that it would have been in the great interest of anyone who wished to disprove the truth of the resurrection to present evidence to the contrary at the time of the publication of the story, and yet no such writing or other evidence has ever been forthcoming. In the face of silence from the authorities in Jerusalem, the message of the resurrection began to be preached passionately and publicly by the apostle Peter and others seven weeks after the crucifixion of Jesus (Acts 2:14–36).[13] All four Gospels report that on the third day after Jesus was buried in the tomb of Joseph of Arimathea, the tomb was empty. This fact is critical to the story of the resurrection, and it is a fact which was easily verifiable by authorities in Jerusalem, yet no one came forward to show that the body was in the tomb, and no body was ever produced from any other source.[14] From this silence, the jury may reasonably infer that the tomb was empty.

It has been suggested, with no supporting evidence, that perhaps the tomb of Jesus was found empty because the body was stolen by his followers. Of course, if there had been any evidence of this, it would have been offered. Additionally, for followers of Jesus to secretly remove the body and then maintain the story of the resurrection would be an act of deliberate deception in conflict with all of the evidence presented to the jury in this case regarding the character of that group of people, particularly Matthew, Mark (or Peter), Luke, and John. Such a deceit would have no basis in logic since we have seen that these same people died for their belief that the resurrection actually occurred. As we have recognized before, people do not die to support a deception.

In fact, the Jewish leaders in Jerusalem were aware that Jesus had predicted his death and resurrection three days later, and therefore specific precautions were taken to prevent his followers from removing the body in order to fulfill the prophecy. The Greek writer Polybius wrote that in the Roman Army routine procedures included guard duty. It is known that, where circumstances warranted, one of the duties of units posted in the provinces, such as Jerusalem, was to guard corpses of the executed.[15] The Gospel of Matthew recites that the Jewish authorities asked Pilate to place a guard at the tomb of Jesus because they wanted to prevent a deception by the apostles, as they had recalled the prophecy of Jesus that he would rise again in three days (Matt. 27:62–66). For that reason the authorities "went and made the grave secure, and along with the guard they set a seal on the stone" (Matt. 27:66). We know that the custom at that time for sealing a tomb is thought to have been stretching a cord across the stone and sealing each end. Sealing was accomplished by or in the presence of the Roman guards, and it had a special significance that the object sealed was under the protection of Roman law.[16]

Historians have noted that these guards, as representatives of Rome, would have performed their duty to guard the tomb strictly and faithfully. They had no vested interest in the task, and their sole purpose and obligation was to perform their duties as soldiers of Rome. Military discipline was strict at that time. Roman soldiers held high standards of discipline and devotion to duty, and this was strictly enforced by the commander of each unit, who would suffer if the regiment showed up badly.[17] A soldier who abandoned his post of duty was corporally punished or reduced in rank. If this was viewed as willful disobedience, the punishment was death.[18] Notwithstanding that discipline, the stone was removed from the tomb and the tomb was found empty.

Some historians have speculated that perhaps the Jewish temple guard and not Roman guards were placed at the tomb. This does not advance the argument, however. Military discipline of the temple guard was almost as strict as that for the Roman guard. Temple guards were responsible for guarding the gates and courts of the temple. Two hundred forty Levites and thirty priests were responsible for acting as a guard for the temple every night. Periodic checks were performed during the night, and a guard who fell asleep while on duty would be severely beaten. It was also permissible to set on fire the clothes that the culpable guard was wearing. Temple guards on watch were required to maintain their posts standing.[19] It is reasonable to assume that the Jewish temple guard would perform their duties at the tomb of Jesus with strict discipline.

In spite of all of these precautions, it bears repeating that no historical writing or any other evidence exists containing a refutation by the Roman authorities, the guards, the Jewish leaders, or anyone else that the tomb was empty three days after the death and burial of Jesus. The silence is deafening. Since controverting proof would have demolished belief in the resurrection, the failure to respond by those who were enemies of the followers of Jesus in Jerusalem is especially significant. A refutation could have been fatal to Christianity at that time.

It has also been suggested, with no supporting evidence, that perhaps the appearances of Jesus after the crucifixion can be explained by the fact that he did not actually die upon the cross. But, as reported in the Gospels, Pontius Pilate himself required proof of the death of Jesus, and before Joseph of

Arimathea was allowed to remove the body for burial, Pilate inquired of the Roman centurion who had been at the crucifixion as to verification (Mark 15:44–45). The centurion who had been keeping guard at the cross watched Jesus take his last breath and is reported in the Gospels to have said, "Truly this man was the Son of God!" (Mark 15:39).

Many medical experts have confirmed the statement by the apostle John that blood and water flowed from the body of Jesus when he was stabbed with a lance during the crucifixion, and that medical interpretation of the historical evidence indicates that Jesus was dead when taken down from the cross.[20] The detailed eyewitness account of the author is very important; consider how striking it is that this statement was made two thousand years ago when this would not have been within the scope of current medical knowledge, even if the person making the statement had been a medical expert. The implications of this statement could not have been recognized by the witness two thousand years ago when the report was written. It is unreasonable to believe therefore that the observation was fabricated.

Further, the Gospels report that the body was wrapped in spices, in conformance with Jewish custom in those days. The spices were pungent and bitter and were wrapped around the body and over the head and face with linens. The burial preparations are described in each of the four Gospels. The Gospel of John describes the mixture of myrrh and aloes used for that purpose at about one hundred pounds weight (John 19:38–40). The body of a crucified person, such as Jesus, however, would not have been washed.[21] The Jewish law of the first century provided an exception against the removal before burial of blood that issued at the moment of a violent death.[22]

It is ludicrous to suppose that after suffering a night of anxiety so extreme as to cause sweat of blood, no sleep, a lack of food or water, beatings, a scourging, the labor of carrying his own cross to Golgotha, a crucifixion during which he was nailed to a cross for hours and then pierced with a lance, and thereafter being wrapped in one hundred pounds of spices and placed in a cold tomb for the night, that Jesus could have lived. Scourging alone was almost a sentence of death. It was mentioned by Josephus twice as customarily preceding crucifixion. Jesus would have been stripped of his clothes and flogged "until the flesh hung down in bloody shreds."[23]

It is even more ludicrous to suppose that, had he lived, he would have been able to appear on that same day to numerous people in various locations as a healthy, happy, whole person. The village of Emmaus in which an early appearance on the day of the resurrection was reported is more than seven miles from the location of the tomb.

All of the foregoing must be considered by the jury in the context of the evidence presented in this case to support the reliability of the Gospel testimony that the resurrection occurred. We can't have it both ways—either the testimony of the Gospels is false, or Jesus was dead when he was taken from the cross and placed in the tomb, and the tomb was found empty three days later. If the speculation that Jesus was not dead or that the tomb was not empty is accepted, *on what evidence has that conclusion been based?*

What does all of this prove? It is this: rational thought is not based upon the musings of individuals.[24] In order to come to a logical conclusion about an issue or a hypothesis, one is required to support that position with evidence. The historical, documentary, archaeological, and other evidence that has been presented to the jury is sufficient to support by more than a preponderance that the life, death, and resurrection of Jesus as reported in the Gospels actually did occur as a historical fact. No conflicting evidence of even near equivalent weight has been presented in two thousand years. This is a message that can be objectively verified. The case for the reliability of the testimony of our witnesses, and the historical facts of the life, death, and resurrection of Jesus has been proved.

CHAPTER EIGHT

The Verdict

The Christian religion seeks out those who doubt. Some of the most poignant words of the Gospels deal with those who have not been given the gift of faith. We are told that if we seek the answers, we will find them; if we knock, the door will be opened to us. We are told that a shepherd with ninety-nine sheep safely in the fold will leave those ninety-nine sheep to seek out the one that is lost. And we are told that Thomas, the doubting follower of Jesus, was especially provided with evidence of the reality of the resurrection.

When you live with doubt, you have two choices. You may accept that this life is all there is, and that we truly are wildflowers that bloom and die; or you may seek after knowledge, wherever that may lead. If you have read this far, it is most likely that you have already made your choice: you are inquisitive and engaged in a search for truth.

The evidence presented in our search for truth has been measured against objective criteria required for a civil case, but the proof of the truth is compelling even under stricter standards. In the United States the standard of proof in a criminal trial such as that of Darlie Routier, the young mother condemned to death for the murder of her sons, is higher than that required for a civil case. In a criminal trial, the jury must find the defendant guilty beyond a reasonable doubt. Adapting even that higher standard of proof for our purposes, if you, the jury, were to actually hear the testimony in court of not one, but four different witnesses whom you believed to be honest and truthful as to their observation that an event had occurred, would you believe that the event had occurred? Consider further how the testimony would be weighed if each witness was consistent in all material respects with the others, and if collateral details of the testimony were all verified by corroborative evidence. Finally, add to that the circumstantial evidence that many people in the communities in which these witnesses lived changed their conduct in a manner that was consistent with the testimony, and that in effect ratified the accuracy and truth of the testimony. That level of proof is much stronger even than the evidence offered in the *Routier* case, and that is the level of proof that has been presented in this case.

Since the facts are verifiable, the evidence is the cornerstone upon which the truth rests. While you are considering that evidence in order to determine your own verdict, reflect upon the surprising accumulation of information that is available to us today after two thousand years to prove the message of the Gospels. A person is forced to reflect upon whether that is merely coincidence, just luck, or whether the revelations of all of this information at this time are something more. Consider all of the components of care required for preservation of this evidence over that period—the solicitude in the transmission of the words spoken by Jesus and in the copying of the manuscripts, the gentle conservation of fragments remaining from papyrus so easily destroyed, of artifacts, of archaeological evidence preserved through wars, plunder, fire, earthquakes, and in spite of political intent to destroy, the imprint of tender spring flowers on the Shroud of Turin, and the nature of medical observations the importance of which was unknown at the time. The implications of the survival and unearthing of all of this evidence alone are worthy of reflection.

Our search for truth in this case has centered on certain facts. The unique facts of the life, death, and resurrection of Jesus form the basic foundation of the entire Christian religion. But the four Gospels present a more complete message than the mere facts that we have examined, although the message cannot be understood and will not be believed without an understanding of those facts. We have developed those facts, point by point. As the music of Mozart is only a part of its mystery, however, the facts that we have examined are only the basic theme of the Gospels, against which the melody of the rest of the message is to be considered.

It is intriguing to suppose that the music of Mozart drifted to us from another dimension in time and space, that the music cascaded like liquid crystal from an unknown source, providing *hints* of something beyond our physical realm. But the evidence of something transcendent which is given by the complete message of the Gospels is much more than a hint—*it is the melody fully developed*. The fusion of the facts that have been proved with the remainder of the Gospels creates the final work. The facts and the message together weave the musical texture, point against counterpoint, note against note, to create a song of love. The message depends upon the facts, and the facts exist to evidence the message.

Each juror can interpret that message alone by reading the words of the messengers. The Gospels tell us to seek answers for ourselves and to listen—but to be careful how we listen. The unique opportunity provided to us by Matthew, Mark, Luke, and John is the ability to determine the meaning of the message set forth in the Gospels as revealed by the words of Jesus, with reliance upon no intercessor. In rendering our own verdicts, we don't need to depend upon anyone's interpretation of this message; it has been preserved for each of us to read and understand.

Perhaps the message has been sent to us in other times. In the Old Testament, for example, prophecies and disastrous consequences were recorded, but the message did not really survive, and through the years our understanding became distorted. Perhaps, because we kept getting it wrong, the message had to be given again in a way that we could not misunderstand—through agonizing suffering of father and son, and physical death, something we all comprehend. The love held by a parent for a child was clearly recognized as the basis for the ultimate sacrifice as far back as the time of Abraham in the Old Testament. The New Testament reflection of that message is written in the clear, simple narrative of very believable witnesses to the ultimate tragedy—the harmony of suffering between the father and the son, like the string of one musical instrument reacting sympathetically to the vibration of another nearby so that the first reverberates when the second cries out.[1] The son was sacrificed and then returned to life in recognizable form so that we could know of the love that is offered to us and the hope of eternal life.

The love inspired by the Gospels is pure love which transcends the lesser rewards of happiness, comfort, or material gain—it is *agape*. *Agape* is love which is one-way and consumes all other options, including reward. It underlies the crucifixion of Jesus of Nazareth. It is present in the love reflected in the surrender of the last seat in a lifeboat. It is the unexplained missing element in most philosophies of the world, from Ayn Rand through Kant and Nietzsche back to Plato, that causes a person to act in a way that cannot be explained by tracing it ultimately to a self-satisfying or material reward outweighing the cost of the action itself. This love is pure and eternal, and its expression through the crucifixion of Jesus offers us hope and comfort.

In a vision of desolation from the Old Testament, a prophet was set down in the midst of a valley filled with dry bones of those who had lost all hope that life had meaning. In Judea at that time, cynicism and bitterness ruled. But God reached out to those hopeless ones, and then "bone came to its bone . . . sinews were on them, and flesh grew, and skin covered them." The breath of God, the spirit within them, then brought them to life, "and they stood on their feet, an exceedingly great army" (Ezek. 37:7–10).

Today many of us live in that valley. We look for meaning and purpose in the glitter of materiality and crystals of the new age, and we bypass the simple evidence that was preserved for us by the messengers two thousand years ago. If we think of it at all, we tell ourselves that this is because the message of Christianity requires belief in a bodily resurrection that we can't understand, but that ignores the fact that we quite readily accept the truth of many things in the world today that we don't understand.

If you, the juror, are able to set aside preconceptions and look to the evidence, bypassing speculation and theory—you may find the simple truth for yourself. It is written in the Gospels. The words of the Gospels do not offer us a mere philosophy. They offer us an understanding of the real meaning and purpose of life. The peace which is offered by the words of our witnesses is not measured by standards of this world, nor can it be explained by philosophers. Unlike philosophy, the truth of the Gospels can be known not merely by human analysis or through logic but because that truth rests upon knowable facts, and evidence sufficient for proof has been carefully preserved. In his own testimony, the apostle John left these words for us: "He who has seen has borne witness, and his witness is true; and he knows that he is telling the truth, so that you also may believe" (John 19:35). And Jesus has said that truth shall set you free.

Then from the four winds will come the breath of God, the breath of life. The valley of dry bones will be left behind. Your own reading of the gospel message will flesh out your verdict. The messengers have told us that comfort is offered to those who seek. Come to me with your sorrows and burdens, Jesus has said, and I will help you bear them.

Now the courtroom is quiet; daylight fades. The jury will withdraw to consider the evidence upon which the verdict must be based. If your verdict is that the facts at issue in this case are more likely than not true, you have a basis for further inquiry into the complete message of the Gospels. It is admitted that many stories in the Gospels have not been examined under the standards applied to the issues in this case. But perhaps that remaining testimony should be viewed in light of the fact of the credibility of the witnesses and the resurrection that they observed. The resurrection can provide a foundation for faith in other things that you may not understand. This is not blind faith. It is faith based upon rationality and careful study, not upon speculation or the whim of interpreters.

As you reflect upon the evidence and your verdict, think of the beauty in the world and what it may mean. Look to the starry, starry nights and observe the order and design of nature. Listen to the whisper of the wind, the music of Mozart, and then listen to the message of the Gospels. The message of the Gospels is that love is the ultimate measure of good. If you listen with discernment, you may hear the full melody.

Endnotes

Introduction
1. Sarah Boxer, "Science Confronts the Unknowable," *New York Times,* Jan. 24, 1998, p. A15. The Alfred P. Sloan Foundation was the grantor.
2. W. Browne, "Physicists Study the Honeybee for Clues to Complex Problems," *New York Times,* April 7, 1998, p. B14.

Chapter 1
1. Darlene Routier was sentenced by a jury to death by injection on February 4, 1997. Even though the evidence was circumstantial and no eyewitnesses were ever found, the jurors took only ten hours to reach a verdict of guilty. See John W. Gonzalez, "Jury orders death penalty for Routier," *Houston Chronicle,* Feb. 5, 1997, p. 1.
2. Federal Rule of Evidence 402.
3. Federal Rule of Evidence 401.
4. Federal Rule of Evidence 401.

5. *McCormick on Evidence* (4th ed.), ed. John W. Strong, vol. 1, Section 185, p. 773.
6. Ibid., p. 777.
7. "General Instructions for Charge," *Pattern Jury Instructions (Civil Cases)*; Prepared by the Committee on Pattern Jury Instructions; District Judges Association, Fifth Circuit. 1997 Edition. West Publishing Co., 1997. Section 3.1; p. 31.
8. John W. Gonzalez, *Houston Chronicle*, Feb. 1, 1997, p. 29.
9. These instructions are based upon *Pattern Jury Instructions* for the Fifth Circuit Federal Court of Appeals. In a civil case where a party may ultimately be deprived of individual rights, for example, termination of parental rights, evidence may be required to be "clear and convincing," a slightly higher standard. See *McCormick on Evidence* (4th ed.), vol. 2, Section 340, p. 442.
10. John Noble Wilford, "Wary Astronomers Ponder an Accelerating Universe," *New York Times*, March 3, 1998, p. B11.

Chapter 2

1. Philip Wesley Comfort, ed., *The Origin of the Bible* (Tyndale House Publishers, Inc., 1992), 181, 195.
2. Ibid., 183.
3. Ibid., 180, 190–91.
4. Bruce Manning Metzger, *The Text of the New Testament* (Oxford University Press, 1968), 34; also see: F. F. Bruce, *The New Testament Documents: Are They Reliable?* (InterVarsity Press, 1997, 5th rev. ed.), 16–17.
5. In legal terminology "hearsay" is an oral statement or a written assertion (and sometimes conduct) other than one made by the declarant while testifying at the trial or hearing, offered in evidence to prove the truth of the matter asserted. See Federal Rule of Evidence 801.
6. Federal Rule of Evidence 803 (16).
7. Federal Rule of Evidence 901(b)(8).
8. *Compton v. Davis Oil Co.*, 607 F. Supp. 1221, 1229 (Dist. Of Wyoming, 1985).
9. "The Epistle of Ignatius to the Tarsians," in *The Ante-Nicene Fathers*, vol. 1, ed. A. Cleveland Coxe (Wm. B. Eerdmans Publishing Company, 1986), 107.

Endnotes

10. Seutonius, "Suet. Vita Claudii, xxv.4," in *Documents of the Christian Church*, selected and edited by Henry Bettenson (Oxford University Press, 1963. Second Edition), p. 2. Also see: A. N. Wilson, *Paul: The Mind of the Apostle* (W.W. Norton & Company, 1997), pp. 94–106.

11. *Paul: The Mind of the Apostle*, pp. 99–100.

12. Tacitus, "Annales, xv.44. The Neronian Persecution," in *Documents of the Christian Church*, 2.

13. Ibid.

14. Pliny (the Younger), "Plin. Epp.x (Ad. Traj.), xcvi," in *Documents of the Christian Church*, p. 3.

15. Ibid.

16. George F. Jowett, *The Drama of the Lost Disciples* (London: Covenant Publishing Co., Ltd., 1970).

17. *The Text of the New Testament*, p. 18.

18. Ibid., p. 29.

19. *Threadgill v. Armstrong World Industries*, 928 F.2d 1366, 1375 (3rd Cir., 1991).

20. *Pettingell v. Boynton*, 139 Mass. 244, 29 N.E. 655 (1885); *Bell v. Brewster*, 44 Ohio 690, 10 N.E. 679 (1887).

21. Weinstein's *Federal Evidence: Commentary on Rules of Evidence for the United States Courts*, 2nd ed. (1998), vol. 5, Section 901.10(2)(a).

22. Federal Rule of Evidence 803 (16). Also see *Weinstein's Federal Evidence*, vol. 5, section 803(21)(2); *McCormick on Evidence*, vol. 2, section 323.

23. *Ship of Gold in the Deep Blue Sea* by Gary Kinder (Atlantic Monthly Press, 1998) is an interesting non-fiction account of this tragedy.

24. *Columbus-America Discovery Group, Inc. v. The Unidentified, Wrecked and Abandoned Sailing Vessel*, 742 F.Supp. 1327 (E.D. Va. 1990); rev'd. on other grounds, 974 F.2d 450 (4th Cir. 1992). Also see: *George v. The Celotex Corporation*, 914 F.2d 26 (2nd. Cir. 1990) where the Court permitted introduction of a report over twenty years under the ancient documents exception, to show the state of the art with respect to knowledge in the asbestos industry as to the safety of a particular level of contamination.

25. *Weinstein's Federal Evidence*, vol. 5, Section 803.21(3).

26. See generally: Joseph A. Wickes, "Ancient Documents and Hearsay," 8 *Tex. L. Rev.* 451, 473 (1930).
27. Federal Rule of Evidence 803 (16), 901 (b)8; *Threadgill v. Armstrong World Industries, Inc.*, 928 F.2d 1366 (3rd Cir. 1991).
28. Federal Rule of Evidence 1004(1).
29. Federal Rule of Evidence 1003.
30. *McCormick on Evidence*, at Section 223, p. 47. The preferable and majority view is that satisfaction of the ancient document exception authenticates an ancient copy of an original writing.
31. *The Text of the New Testament*, p. 19.
32. Norman L. Geisler and William E. Nix, *A General Introduction to the Bible* (Moody Press, 1986), 466.
33. *A General Introduction to the Bible*, p. 475.
34. *A General Introduction to the Bible*, p. 474; quoting Brooke Foss Westcott and Fenton John Anthony Hart, *The New Testament in the Original Greek*; Benjamin B. Warfield, *An Introduction to the Textual Criticism of the Bible* (London: 1886), p. 13–14.
35. *The New Testament Documents: Are They Reliable?*, p. 19.
36. Frederick G. Kenyon, *Our Bible and the Ancient Manuscripts* (Harper & Brothers, 1941), 23; also see *The Origin of the Bible*, p. 182.
37. *The Origin of the Bible*, p. 200.
38. Conclusion of Philip Comfort in *The Origin of the Bible*, pp. 199–204.
39. Charles Pellegrino, *Return to Sodom and Gomorrah* (Avon Books, 1994), p. 324.
40. Ibid., p. 324.
41. Simon Greenleaf, *The Testimony of the Evangelists* (Grand Rapids: Kregel, 1995), p. 18. (Original publication was in 1874.)

Chapter 3

1. Federal Rule of Evidence 602.
2. *Weinstein's Federal Evidence*, vol. 3, Section 602.03(1)a).
3. *Kansas City Power & Light Co. v. Ford Motor Credit Co.*, 995 F.2d 1422, 1432 (8th Cir. 1993).
4. *Folio Impressions, Inc. v. Byer California*, 752 F.Supp. 583, 586-587 (S.D.N.Y. 1990), aff'd. 937 F.2d 759 (2nd Cir. 1991).
5. *United States v. Quezada*, 754 F.2d 1190, 1195-1196 (5th Cir. 1985).

Endnotes

6. *Senecal v. Drolette*, 304 N.Y. 446, 108 N.E. 2d 602 (Court of Appeals, New York, 1952).
7. Leading proponents of this theory include Dr. Albert Schweitzer, E. P. Sanders, and Burton Mack, as well as the fellows of the Jesus Seminar, including Marcus J. Borg and John Dominic Crosson.
8. James H. Charlesworth, *Jesus and the Dead Sea Scrolls* (Doubleday, 1992), xxxiii. This test has confirmed the archeological, historical, and paleographical methods of assigning dates to the scrolls.
9. Flavius Josephus, "Wars of the Jews," book 5, chap. 11, (1), in *The Complete Works of Josephus*, trans. William Whiston, A.M. (Kregel Publications, 1981), p. 565.
10. Flavius Josephus, "Wars of the Jews," book 5, chap. 12, (3), in *The Complete Works of Josephus*, p. 568.
11. Tacitus "Annales. Xv.44," in *Documents of the Christian Church*, p. 2.
12. Flavius Josephus, "Antiquities of the Jews," bk. 20, chap. 9, in *The Complete Works of Josephus*, p. 423.
13. John A. T. Robinson, *Redating the New Testament* (The Westminster Press, 1976), p. 103.
14. Ibid., p. 104.
15. Ibid., p. 311.
16. See Carsten Peter Thiede and Matthew D'Ancona, *Eyewitness to Jesus* (Doubleday, 1996).
17. Ibid., p. 27.
18. Ibid, pp. 56–57. The fact that these early dated fragments also include narrative portions of the Gospel of Matthew and quotations from persons other than Jesus also significantly undermines a similar theory of many biblical scholars that the entire Gospel was written at a much later period of time based upon a few "sayings" or quotations from Jesus (but without any narration or quotations from others) which had been preserved through the years from the first century A.D. The full text of both sides of each of the Magdalen fragments, translated into English and reprinted by Thiede is as follows:

Fragment 1: "poured it on his head as he was at table. When the disciples saw this, they said indignantly"

179

Fragment 2: "Jesus noticed this and said, 'Why are you upsetting this woman? What she has done for me . . .'"

Fragment 3: "Then one of the twelve, the man called Judas Iscariot, went to the chief priests and said, 'What are you prepared to give me . . .'"

Fragment 3: "They were greatly distressed and started asking him in turn, 'Not me, Lord, surely?' He answered, 'Someone who has dipped his hand into the dish with me . . .'"

Fragment 1: "Jesus said to them, 'You will all fall away from me tonight, for the scripture says . . .'"

Fragment 2: "I shall go ahead of you to Galilee. At this, Peter said to him"

Translations are as quoted in the New Jerusalem Bible, *Eyewitness to Jesus*, p. 56.

19. *Eyewitness to Jesus*, pp. 64–65.
20. Ibid., p. 71.
21. *A General Introduction to the Bible*, p. 352.
22. In *Eyewitness to Jesus*, Thiede has also credited earlier recognition of the similarities between these two sets of early dated fragments to Peter Weignadt and Kurt Aland in reports written in 1966.
23. *Eyewitness to Jesus*, p. 119.
24. Ibid., pp. 68–70.
25. Ibid., p. 70.
26. Ibid., p. 124.
27. Ibid., p. 35.
28. Ibid., p. 35.
29. Ibid., pp. 60–61.
30. It has also been reported that nineteen small fragments of the Gospel of Mark found among the Dead Sea Scrolls have been identified and assigned a date of around A.D. 50 by Professor Jose O'Callaghan, of the Pontifical Biblical Institute in Rome. See *Search for the Twelve Apostles*, p. 251.
31. *Eyewitness to Jesus*, p. 111.
32. Ibid., p. 109.
33. Ibid., pp. 36–46.
34. As noted in *Eyewitness to Jesus*, p. 36.

Endnotes

35. As quoted in *Eyewitness to Jesus*, p. 32.
36. *Eyewitness to Jesus*, pp. 17–18.
37. *Redating the New Testament*, pp. 254–311.
38. Ian Wilson, *Jesus: The Evidence* (HarperSanFrancisco, 1996), 93–94.
39. Ibid., p. 93.
40. Jack Finegan, *The Archeology of the New Testament* (Princeton University Press, 1992), 193. In fact, the *entire* temple complex, including many other buildings surrounding the temple, was not completed until approximately thirty years later.
41. *Origins of the Bible*, p. 72; also see Raymond E. Brown, *An Introduction to the New Testament* (Doubleday, 1997), 368.
42. *An Introduction to the New Testament*, p. 368.
43. *Redating the New Testament*, p. 307.
44. Compilation of Scripture taken from Josh McDowell, *Evidence that Demands a Verdict* (Thomas Nelson Publishers, 1979), 8–9.
45. *The New Testament Documents: Are They Reliable?*, pp. 16–17.
46. *The Text of the New Testament*, p. 34.
47. *The Testimony of the Evangelists*, p. 18.
48. See *Did Jesus Rise from the Dead: The Resurrection Debate*, ed. Terry L. Miethe (Harper & Row, 1987), 23, 55, 86; also see *The New Testament Documents: Are They Reliable?*, p. 76.
49. See *Redating of the New Testament*, p. 96.
50. Bruce A. Metzger, *The Canon of the New Testament* (Clarendon Press, 1987); also see *The Origin of the Bible*, p. 69.
51. Gary R. Habermas, *Ancient Evidence for the Life of Jesus* (Thomas Nelson Publishers, 1984), 141.
53. *The Origin of the Bible*, p. 71. Philip Comfort reports that a writing known as the *Gospel of Truth*, probably written by Valentinus, refers to the Gospels, Acts, letters of Paul, Hebrews, and the Book of Revelation, treating them as authoritative and indicating that a compilation was in existence at that time.
53. "Fragments of Papias," in *The Ante-Nicene Fathers*, vol. 1, p. 155. Five writings of Papias are preserved by other ancient writers, and these are referred to as the *Oracles of the Lord*.
54. *An Introduction to the New Testament*, p. 212, n 91.
55. Irenaeus, "Adversus haereses, III. I.i " (preserved in Euseb. H.E. V.8); in *Documents of the Christian Church*, p. 28.

56. For a general discussion, see *Introduction to the New Testament,* pp. 209–210; also see the unsupported premise of the fellows of The Jesus Seminar in *The Five Gospels* that Papias's assertion was "patently false," and in complete disregard for the evidence, further stating that Matthew was first composed in Greek in dependence upon the mysterious document referred to as Q, believed to contain nothing more than a few "sayings" of Jesus preserved from the first century (*The Five Gospels,* translation and commentary by Robert W. Funk, Roy W. Hoover, and The Jesus Seminar [HarperSan Francisco, 1997], 20).

57. Eusebius, "The Epistles of Ignatius," in William Stewart McBirnie, *The Search for the Twelve Apostles* (Living Books, Tyndale House Publishers, Inc., 1973), 53.

58. "Fragments of Papias," in *The Ante-Nicene Fathers,* vol. 1, p. 153. Also see *The New Testament Documents,* p. 29.

59. Eusebius, HE 3.39.1, quoting Irenaeus, Adv. Haer. 5.33–34. Cited in *Redating The New Testament,* p. 95.

60. The reference is preserved in a fragment taken from Anastasius Sinaita, as given in "Fragments of Papias," in the *Ante-Nicene Fathers,* vol. 1, p. 155, f.n. 3. Reference from the *Anti-Marcionite Prologue* is found in *The New Testament Documents,* p. 52.

61. *The Search for the Twelve Apostles,* p. 175.

62. *An Introduction to the New Testament,* p. 210, n. 86; Brown, however, adds a personal qualifier that it is possible that this acceptance may have been based upon the fact that they had never questioned the tradition of the existence of an original Aramaic manuscript.

63. See *The New Testament Documents,* pp. 38–39; but see *Introduction to the New Testament,* p. 210.

64. "Fragments of Papias," in *The Ante-Nicene Fathers,* vol. 1, p. 155. Also see F. F. Bruce. *The New Testament Documents: Are They Reliable?,* p. 35.

65. Irenaeus, "Adversus haereses, III.I.i" (Euseb. H.E. V.8), in *Documents of the Christian Church,* p. 28. Also see *Redating the New Testament,* pp. 110–111.

66. *Redating the New Testament,* p. 108.

67. *"Fragments from Cassiodorus"* (a Latin translation by Cassidorus of fragments of Clement of Alexandria on Comments on the First

Epistle of Peter), in *The Ante-Nicene Fathers,* vol. 2, p. 573. Also see: *Redating the New Testament,* p. 109. In this quote from 1 Peter 5:13, the apostle also refers to his "son, Mark."

68. *The New Testament Documents,* pp. 35–36.
69. Ibid., p. 37.
70. C. H. Turner, "Marcian Usage," *Journal of Theological Studies,* in *The New Testament Documents,* p 36.
71. *New Testament Documents,* pp. 36–37.
72. *The Testimony of the Evangelists,* p. 22; also see *The New Testament Documents,* p. 36.
73. See *The Search for the Twelve Apostles,* pp. 252–253; also see *Eyewitness to Jesus,* p. 13.
74. *U.S. v. DaSilva,* 725 F.2d 828 (2nd Cir. 1983); also see *U.S. v. Alvarez,* 755 F.2d 830, 859-860 (11th Cir. 1985) *cert. den.* 474 U.S. 905.
75. Irenaeus, "Adversus haereses, X.I.i." (Euseb. H.E. V.8), in *Documents of the Christian Church,* p. 28.
76. *An Introduction to the New Testament,* p. 267.
77. *Redating the New Testament,* p. 101.
78. For a detailed compilation of New Testament sources for this information, see *The New Testament Documents,* pp. 41–42.
79. *Eyewitness to Jesus,* p. 70.
80. *The New Testament Documents: Are They Reliable?,* p. 47.
81. Ibid., p. 48–50.
82. Ibid., p. 50; also see *Introduction to the New Testament,* p. 368. For a description of the persecution of Polycarp, see "The Martyrdom of Polycarp," in *Documents of the Christian Church,* p. 9.
83. *The New Testament Documents: Are They Reliable?,* p. 51.
84. Irenaeus, "Adversus haereses, III.I.i" (Euseb. H.E. V.8), in *Documents of the Christian Church,* p. 28.
85. *The New Testament Documents,* p. 52; quoting from the Anti-Marcionite Prologue to the Gospel of John. The prologue was referred to as Anti-Marcionite because it opposed the views of Marcion, who lived in Rome in approximately A.D. 140. Maricon created the earliest list, or canon, of the New Testament books, but was labeled a heretic because of his theological position supporting rejection of the entire Old Testament in favor of the New Testament.

86. *The New Testament Documents: Are They Reliable?*, p. 50.
87. James H. Charlesworth, *Jesus and the Dead Sea Scrolls* (Doubleday, 1992), xxxiii.
88. For examples, see *Jesus and the Dead Sea Scrolls*, p. xxxiv; also see *The New Testament Documents: Are They Reliable?*, p. 58: and *Jesus the Evidence*, pp. 34, 35.
89. *Redating the New Testament*, p. 284. Robinson has compared the style of the Gospel of John favorably to the Books of Colossians, Jude, and 2 Peter.
90. Federal Rule of Evidence 701.
91. *United States Equal Employment Opportunity Commission and Adetunji Adebayo v. Catholic Knights Insurance Society*, 915 F. Supp. 25, 27 (Northern District of Illinois; 1996), construing Federal Rule of Evidence 602; Advisory Committee's Note.
92. See *U.S. v. Alvarez*; *U.S. v. DaSilva*.
93. See *The New Testament Documents: Are They Reliable?* for a discussion of this research.
94. *Nationwide Mutual Insurance Co. v. Darden*, 503 U.S. 318, 112 S. Ct. 1344, 1349, 117 L.Ed. 3d 581 (1992), (setting forth the common law test for determination of an agency relationship); *Pappas v. Middle Earth Condominium Assn.*, 963 F.2d 534 (2nd Cir. 1992).
95. *Matthews Roofing v. Community Bank & Trust Company of Edgewater*, 194 Ill. App. 3d 200, 206, 550 N.E. 2d 1189, 1193, 141 Ill. (1990); *American Laser Products, Inc. v. National Imaging Supplies Group, Inc.*, No. 94 C 7624 (1st Dist. 1996), LEXIS 3520 (1996), p. 55. (An agency relationship need not depend on an express appointment, but may be created by the situation of the parties, their actions, and other relevant circumstances.) Also see *Pappias v. Middle Earth Condominium Assn.*, p. 538 (agency may be proved by circumstantial evidence); *Wargel v. First National Bank of Harrisburg*, 121 Ill. App. 3d 730, 460 N.E. 331, 334, 77 Ill. Dec. 275 (5th Dist. 1984) (an agency relationship must be determined by analyzing the parties' actual practices).
96. *Testimony of the Evangelists*, p. 25.
97. Ibid., p. 26.
98. Federal Rule of Evidence 804(b)(4)(B).
99. *McCormick on Evidence*, vol. 1, Section 10, p. 40.

Endnotes

Chapter 4

1. *The New Testament Documents: Are They Reliable?*, pp. 34–35, particularly Theodor von Zahn, Dom B. C. Butler and Dom John Chapman.
2. Eusebius, "H.E. iii. 39," in *The New Testament Documents*, p. 38; for a general discussion of this issue, see *The New Testament Documents: Are They Reliable?*, pp. 32–38.
3. *Introduction to the New Testament*, p. 209.
4. The fellows of the Jesus Seminar have taken the position that a work referred to as the "Gospel of Thomas" evidences the existence of a Q document, because the Gospel of Thomas contains no narrative and is composed solely of quotations, or "sayings" of Jesus. Clearly the Gospel of Thomas itself does not evidence the Q document because it is dated much later than the Gospels, even considering the most conservative orthodox dating. The Coptic version of this work was found in 1946 in Egypt together with a group of texts, referred to as the Nag Hammadi texts. These are codices believed by most scholars to be dated to the third and fourth centuries A.D., although Greek fragments of a version of this Gospel may be dated as early as the end of the second century. They reflect the thinking of a very unorthodox group of people living in the second century, commonly referred to as Gnostics. Although these texts are important in that they show the beginnings of wide acceptance of the teachings of Christianity at that period of time, many scholars do not believe that they offer any new understanding of the New Testament. See F. F. Bruce, *The New Testament Documents: Are They Reliable?*, p. 98. For a contrary view that appears to be based solely on speculation, see *The Five Gospels*, translation and commentary by Robert W. Funk, Roy W. Hoover, and the Jesus Seminar (Harper San Francisco, Harper Collins Publishers, 1993).
5. For a discussion, see *The New Testament Documents: Are They Reliable?*, pp. 31–32.
6. *Eyewitness to Jesus*, p. 135.
7. The text was found in the Wadi Muraba, inventory and plate number 164 (*Eyewitness to Jesus*, p. 137).
8. Ibid., p. 136.
9. The comparison is suggested by F. F. Bruce in *The New Testament Documents: Are They Reliable?*, p. 32.

10. *Gospel Parallels: A Synopsis of the First Three Gospels,* 4th ed., Burton H. Throckmorton Jr. (Thomas Nelson Inc., 1979).

11. Matt. 27:58; Mark 15:43; Luke 23:52, as quoted from the 4th ed. of *Gospel Parallels.*

12. *The Precise Parallel New Testament,* ed. John R. Kohlenberger III (Oxford University Press, 1995).

13. See *Gospel Parallels.*

14. *Gospel Parallels,* pp. 171, 175, 177, 183, 185, setting forth corresponding passages in Luke 22:52 (a portion of the sentences), 61 (quotation only, contained in the last sentence of this passage); 22:62 (entire sentence); 23:3 and 23:44 (a portion of a sentence), 23:52 (a portion of a sentence).

15. Some authorities believe that the original Gospel of Mark ended with verse 16:8, in which various women followers of Jesus are reported to have visited the tomb three days after the burial of Jesus, only to find the tomb empty and an announcement by a young man (implicitly an angel messenger) that he has risen from the dead. In that case, presumably the original manuscript would not have included descriptions of post-resurrection visits included in the other Gospels, although it would have contained an announcement of the resurrection. However, other scholars believe that the original Gospel included the more extensive ending generally given in modern Bibles, and some support for that is found in some of the early manuscripts which do, in fact, contain an ending with post-resurrection reports. See *An Introduction to the New Testament,* p. 148.

16. For a general discussion of the topical arrangements, see Darrell L. Bock, "The Words of Jesus in the Gospels: Live, Jive, or Memorex?," in *Jesus Under Fire,* ed. Michael J. Wilkins and J. P. Moreland (Zondervan Publishing House, 1995), 84–89.

17. *Testimony of the Evangelists,* pp. 22–23.

Chapter 5

1. *McCormick on Evidence,* vol. 2, Section 339; p. 436.

2. *Testimony of the Evangelists,* p. 31.

3. *McCormick on Evidence,* vol. 1, Section 34, p. 111, note 1 (quoting Tribe, "Triangulating Hearsay," 87 *Harv. L. Rev.* 957, 1974).

4. The Book of Acts and many other writings of the New Testament chronicle Peter's position as a leader of the early church. Writings

of Eusebius also refer to the leadership of Peter throughout the entire area, and Polycarp's succession to that position at Smyrna in Asia during this turbulent time. For an interesting and full discussion, see *The Search for the Twelve Apostles,* pp. 52–67.

5. *The Search for the Twelve Apostles,* pp. 72–75. In 1968 Pope Paul announced that the bones of Peter and the grave had been located. In 1971 *National Geographic* reported that the bones had also been found, and at that time were hidden from the public in a niche in the tomb. Aubrey Minion, "St. Peter's," *National Geographic,* December 1971, vol. 140, no. 6, pp. 872–873.

6. Federal Rules of Evidence 404(a) and 608; see Notes of Advisory Committee on Proposed Rules to Rule 608(a) regarding the exception under Rule 404(a) for admissibility of character evidence of a witness as bearing upon his or her credibility; also see *McCormick on Evidence,* vol. 1, Section 187.

7. Federal Rule of Evidence 405(b).

8. Federal Rule of Evidence 608(b).

9. *Compton v. Davis Oil Co.,* 607 F. Supp. 1221, 1228, 1230 (D.C. Wyoming. 1985). Here the court stated that it was persuaded of the truth of recitals contained in a death certificate introduced into evidence under the ancient document exception concerning a common law marriage because of the fact that the conduct of the heirs of the married couple and declarations of relatives regarding their marital status over the course of many years was fully consistent with such recitals.

10. Federal Rule of Evidence 405(a).

11. Ignatius, "Epistle of Ignatius to the Trallians," in *The Ante-Nicene Fathers,* vol. I, p. 70.

12. Ibid.

13. *Rex v. Woodcock,* 1 Leach 500, 168 Eng. Rep. 352 (K.B. 1789); see *McCormick on Evidence,* vol. 2; Section 310, pp. 325–331.

14. *Testimony of the Evangelists,* p. 33.

15. Federal Rule of Evidence 601.

16. Ibid.

17. Neil Asher Silberman, "Searching For Jesus," *Archaeology,* November-December 1994, vol. 4, pp. 30–40.

18. William Barclay, *The Gospel of Luke,* rev. ed. (The Westminster Press, 1975), 52.

19. See *Jesus: The Evidence*, p. 124, quoting Dr. Frederick Zugibe, a forensic pathologist and chief medical examiner of Rockland County, New York.

20. This aspect of the nature of Jesus is noted by Wilson, in *Jesus: The Evidence*, pp. 54–55.

21. Werner Keller, *The Bible as History* (William Morrow and Company, Inc., 1981), 323–24; also see William Barclay, *The Gospel of Luke* (The Westminster Press, 1975), 20.

22. *Jesus: The Evidence*, p. 48. The Roman census order was found in Egypt and dates from A.D. 104 during the reign of the emperor Trajan. It is analogous to the one described in the Gospel of Luke. Also see *The Gospel of Luke*, p. 21.

23. Eric M. Meyers, "Galilee in the Time of Jesus," *Archeology*, November-December 1994, p. 41; also see Neil Asher Silberman, "Searching for Jesus," *Archaeology*, vol. 47; November–December, 1994, pp. 30–40.

24. The discovery is best described in Jack Finegan, *Archeology of the New Testament* (Princeton University Press, 1991), 82; for pictures of the excavated fishing boat, see *Jesus: The Evidence*, pp. 80–83.

25. *The Archeology of the New Testament*, p. 82.

26. William Barclay, *The Gospel of John* (The Westminster Press, 1975), vol. 2, pp. 52–57.

27. *Testimony of the Evangelists*, p. 47.

28. Ibid., p. 34.

29. The theorem has been paraphrased in English as follows: "All consistent axiomatic formulations of number theory include undecidable propositions." See Douglas R. Hofstadter, *Godel, Escher, Bach: An Eternal Golden Braid* (Vintage Books, 1980), p. 17 for a brilliant explanation of the theorem.

30. Roger Penrose, *Shadows of the Mind: A Search for the Missing Science of Consciousness* (Oxford University Press, 1994), 72.

31. See David J. Chalmers, *The Conscious Mind: In Search of a Fundamental Theory* (Oxford University Press, 1996); *Shadows of the Mind: A Search for the Missing Science of Consciousness*.

32. See Paul Davies, *The Mind of God: The Scientific Basis for a Rational World* (Touchstone, Simon & Schuster, 1992), 50; Stephen W. Hawking, *A Brief History of Time: From the Big Bang to Black Holes* (Bantam Books, 1988).

Endnotes

33. For a general discussion of the scientific basis for these statements, see Patrick Glynn, *God: The Evidence* (Prima Publishing, 1997); Paul Davies, *The Mind of God;* Hugh Ross, *The Creator and the Cosmos* (NavPress, 1993); *A Brief History of Time.*
34. See Hubert P. Yockey, *Information Theory and Molecular Biology* (Cambridge University Press, 1992), p. 257.
35. Ibid., p. 242.
36. See Charles B. Thaxton, Walter L. Bradley, Roger L. Olsen, *The Mystery of Life's Origin* (Lewis and Stanley, 1984, 1992).
37. Robert Shapiro, *Origins: A Skeptic's Guide to the Creation of Life on Earth* (Summit Books 1986), 104. Robert Shapiro is a professor of chemistry at New York University. He is a leading authority on origin of life research and has written several books on the subject.
38. Ibid., p. 116.
39. Charles B. Thaxton, Walter L. Bradley, Roger L. Olsen, *The Mystery of Life's Origin: Reassessing Current Theories* (Lewis and Stanley, 1984, 1992). Chemical evolution is described by the authors as "the pre-biological phase of evolution in which the very earliest living things came into being." For an excellent overall discussion, see *Origins: A Skeptic's Guide to the Creation of Life on Earth,* by Robert Shapiro.
40. See Michael Behe, *Darwin's Black Box: The Biochemical Challenge to Evolution* (The Free Press, a division of Simon & Schuster, Inc., 1996), for a discussion of "irreducibly complex" biochemical systems of the human organism.
41. The existence of such matter, derived from indirect, circumstantial evidence, was most recently confirmed by results from the Cosmic Background Explorer (COBE) satellite announced on April 24, 1992. For a discussion of these results, see Hugh Ross, *The Creator and the Cosmos* (NavPress, 1993), pp. 29–31.
42. Heisenberg's uncertainty principle holds that the position and the momentum of any subatomic particle cannot be known or measured simultaneously.
43. Simon Singh, "The Proof Is in the Neutrino," *The New York Times,* June 16, 1998, p. A31. Physicists in Japan now have demonstrated that the neutrino has mass.
44. "New Findings Suggest Massive Black Holes Lurk in the Hearts of Many Galaxies," *New York Times,* January 14, 1997, p. B9; also

189

see *A Brief History of Time* and *The Creator and the Cosmos.*
Observations by the Hubble telescope have proved compelling evidence for the reality of black holes, and most scientists now accept that they exist.
45. Ibid.
46. *Testimony of the Evangelists,* p. 38.

Chapter 6
1. Ibid., p. 39.
2. Ibid., p. 40.
3. Ibid.
4. Ibid., p. 43.
5. Chalmers, *Evidences of the Christian Revelation,* American ed., quoted in *Testimony of the Evangelists,* p. 44.
6. Tacitus, *"Annales xv:44,"* in *Documents of the Christian Church,* pp. 1–2.
7. Seutonius, "Suet. Vita Claudii, xxv.4," in *Documents of the Christian Church,* p. 2. Seutonius was a Roman historian under the emperor Hadrian.
8. Pliny (the Younger), "Epp. X (ad Traj.), xcvi," in *Documents of the Christian Church,* p. 3.
9. Ibid., pp. 3–4.
10. *The New Testament Documents: Are They Reliable?,* p. 113.
11. Flavius Josephus, *Antiquities of the Jews,* bk. 18; chap. 3 (3). Reprinted in *The Complete Works of Josephus.*
12. The monograph in Arabic was published by an Israeli scholar in 1971. See *Jesus Under Fire,* p. 213. Also see Gary R. Habermas, *Ancient Evidence for the Life of Jesus* (Thomas Nelson Publishers, 1988), 91–92.
13. *Ancient Evidence for the Life of Jesus,* p. 92.
14. Flavius Josephus, *Antiquities of the Jews,* bk. 20, chap. 9 (1), in *The Complete Works of Flavius Josephus,* p. 423.
15. *Ancient Evidence for the Life of Jesus,* p. 98. The Talmud contains several other references which may possibly be references to Jesus of Nazereth; however, many were written centuries later and not all are positive.
16. *The Bible as History,* p. 328–329.
17. *Jesus: The Evidence,* p. 48.

Endnotes

18. Justin Martyr, "Dialogue with the Jew Trypho," *The Archeology of the New Testament*, p. 30.
19. Origen, *"Against Celsus.* I 51," in *The Archeology of the New Testament*, p. 30.
20. *The Archeology of the New Testament*, p. 36.
21. Ibid., pp. 43–49.
22. Ibid., p. 48.
23. Stuart Miller, "Sepphoris, the Well Remembered City," *Biblical Archaeologist,* June 1992, vol. 55; pp. 74–83; Neil Asher Silberman, "Searching for Jesus," *Archaeology* November-December, 1994, vol. 47, pp. 30–40.
24. Stuart S. Miller, "Sepphoris, the Well Remembered City," *Biblical Archaeologist.* Miller noted that this connection was first recognized by Richard A Batey.
25. As noted in *Jesus: The Evidence*, pp. 61–63.
26. *Jesus: The Evidence*, p. 66.
27. Flavius Josephus, *Antiquities of the Jews*, book 18, chap. 5 (2), (4), in *The Complete Works of Josephus.*
28. *The Archeology of the New Testament*, p. 99.
29. Ibid., p. 104. Carbo specifically referred to a reference by Jesus from Luke 7:9 ("I tell you, not even in Israel have I found such faith"). Also see *Jesus: The Evidence*, p. 78.
30. *Jesus: The Evidence*, p. 78.
31. Record of a pilgrimage by Aetheria, quoted by Peter the Deacon (A.D. 381–384). The quote appears in *The Archeology of the New Testament*, p. 110.
32. "We come to Capernaum into the house of St. Peter, which is a basilica." Anonymous of Piacenza, in A.D. 570; quoted in *The Archeology of the New Testament*, p. 110.
33. *The Archeology of the New Testament*, pp. 107–109. The floors of other houses located around the one identified with Peter were of beaten earth or basalt pebbles; in this house the floors were treated with crushed limestone, and its walls were constantly replastered and decorated, evidencing special attention throughout many centuries, back to the first century.
34. *The Archeology of the New Testament*, p. 109; also see *Jesus: The Evidence*, p. 78.
35. *The Archeology of the New Testament*, pp. 109–110; also see

Jesus: The Evidence, p. 79. In the fourth century a new ceiling and additional rooms were added, and the venerated room appears to have begun to be used as a church.

36. Revised from a compilation in *Jesus: The Evidence,* p. 81.
37. *Jesus, The Evidence,* pp. 82–83.
38. Ibid.
39. *The Archeology of the New Testament,* pp. 156–162.
40. Pictures and a description of the excavations are contained in *The Archeology of the New Testament,* p. 158.
41. *The Archeology of the New Testament,* p. 159.
42. Ibid., pp. 81, 82.
43. *Jesus: The Evidence,* p. 82.
44. The Thompson Chain-Reference Bible, New American Standard, p. 2,079.
45. Walter E. Rast, *Through the Ages in Palestinian Archaeology* (Trinity Press International, 1992), 134; also see John Rogerson and Philip Davies, "Siloam Tunnel," *Archaeology,* Sept. 1996, vol. 59, no. 3; "Rejoinder to Rogerson & Davies," *Archaeology,* Dec. 1996, vol. 59, no. 4.
46. Josephus, *Wars of the Jews,* book 5, chap. 5(6), in *The Complete Works of Josephus,* p. 555.
47. *Jesus: The Evidence,* pp. 109–111.
48. Ibid., p. 112.
49. Ibid., pp. 112–113.
50. Eusebius, "Onomasticon," *The Archeology of the New Testament,* p. 175.
51. Account of the pilgrim, Aetheria (381–184) in *The Archeology of the New Testament,* p. 178.
52. *The Archeology of the New Testament,* p. 181.
53. *Jesus: The Evidence,* p. 123.
54. *Searching for Jesus,* p. 38. Also see *Jesus: The Evidence,* pp. 106–107.
55. *Searching for Jesus,* p. 38. Also see *Jesus: The Evidence,* pp. 108, 119.
56. The first reference is in *Antiquities of the Jews,* book 18, chap. 2 (2), in *The Complete Works of Josephus,* p. 378. The second reference is in *Antiquities of the Jews,* book 18, chap. 4(3), in *The Complete Works of Josephus,* p. 381.

Endnotes

57. *Searching for Jesus,* p. 38.
58. *The Archeology of the New Testament,* pp. 138–139; *Searching for Jesus,* p. 40.
59. *The Bible as History,* p. 347.
60. *Jesus: The Evidence,* p. 35.
61. *Searching for Jesus,* p. 40; also see *Jesus and the Dead Sea Scrolls,* p. 279.
62. Belief that the evidence indicated a final "coup de grace" was published by N. Haas in 1970 in the original publication of the findings. This position is also supported by Ian Wilson, in *Jesus: The Evidence,* p. 30. In *Jesus and the Dead Sea Scrolls,* however, Charlesworth has stated his own opinion that the breaks in the leg were due to the passage of time rather than to a single strong blow.
63. Special Communication, William D. Edwards, M.D.; Wesley J. Gabel, M.Div.; Floyd E. Mosmer, M.S., AMI. "On the Physical Death of Jesus Christ," *Journal of the American Medical Association* (March 21, 1986), vol. 255, no. 11, pp. 1455-63. (Dr. Edwards is a physician at the Department of Pathology, Mayo Clinic, Rochester, Minn.) See also, *Ancient Evidence for the Life of Jesus,* p. 58.
64. *The Bible as History,* p. 356.
65. Gilbert R. Lavoie, *Unlocking the Secrets of the Shroud* (Thomas More, 1998), p. 24.
66. Statement by Piero Savarino, professor at Turin University, at a meeting of the non-religious Giovanni Agnelli Foundation meeting of academics in February 1998. From an article by Andrew Gumbel, "Ten Years on the Debunked Turin Shroud Gets a Second Coming," *Independent,* Feb. 1, 1998; also see Walter E. Rast, *Through the Ages in Palestinian Archaeology* (Trinity Press International, 1992), 37–38.
67. Announcement of researchers from University of Texas, Health Science Center, San Antonio, Texas, at a meeting of the American Society of Microbiology, *Newsday,* May 22, 1996 (Associated Press). That conclusion is supported by earlier work in 1994 by Dimitri Kouznetsov, a Russian biochemist, although his research has not yet been confirmed.
68. For a full discussion of the work of Garza-Valdes and the University of Texas, see Ian Wilson, *The Blood and the Shroud* (Free Press, 1998), 223–231.
69. Andrew Gumbel, "Ten Years on the Debunked Turin Shroud Gets a Second Coming," *Independent,* Feb. 1, 1998; Giovanni Agnelli Foundation meeting of Academics in Turin, Italy.

FAITH ON TRIAL

70. "Science Can't Unravel Enigma of Cloth's Age," *Newsday,* Oct. 30, 1994. On the other hand, Ian Wilson, author of *The Blood and the Shroud,* is critical of Kouznetsov on a personal level, and noted that as of the publication of Wilson's book in 1998, Kouznetsov's work has not yet been confirmed and remains somewhat controversial. See *The Blood and the Shroud,* pp. 221–223.
71. *Through the Ages,* pp. 37–38. Many factors affect C-14 in organic matter, for example, changes in the earth's magnetic field and the effects of the sun's activity; C-14 is influenced by amospheric and environmental conditions.
72. John McRay, "Response," *Biblical Archaeologist,* Sept. 1993, vol. 56, no. 3, p. 161; "Expert Says Turin Shroud Older Than Tests Say," *Reuters,* June 10, 1997; Andrew Gumbel, "Ten Years on the Debunked Turin Shroud Gets a Second Coming," *Independent,* Feb. 1, 1998 (conclusion of academics meeting for Giovanni Agnelli Foundation, Turin, Italy).
73. Gilbert R. Lavoie, *Unlocking the Secrets of the Shroud* (Thomas More, 1998), 123.
74. Laurence McQuilian, "Turin Shroud Is as Old as Christ," *Reuters,* July 5, 1996, Turin, Italy. From an announcement by Nello Balossino and Pierluigi Baima Bollone, Turin University. Also see *Colliers Encyclopedia* CD Rom; 28 Feb. 1996.
75. Edward Gibbon, *The Decline and Fall of the Roman Empire,* vol. 2 (Encyclopedia Britannica, Inc. 1952), pp. 196–97; as noted in *Unlocking the Secrets of the Shroud,* p. 49. Also see *The Blood and The Shroud.*
76. For a full chart of the species identified by Max Frei and their particular environs, see *The Blood and the Shroud,* p.102.
77. Announcement of professor Avinoan Darin, expert in plant life in Israel, and Dr. Alan Whanger, medical lecturer, researchers at Hebrew University of Jerusalem and Duke University in North Carolina, respectively; Judy Siegel, "Plant Evidence Supports Authenticity of Shroud of Turin," *Jerusalem Post,* 14th April, 1997; also see Eric Silver, "Discoveries: Flower Evidence Links Turin Shroud to the Holy Land," *Independent,* Dec. 8, 1997. Professor Avinoam Danin stated that "[T]he fact that the images of winter leaves appear on the shroud together with the previous year's petioles [a stalk joining the leaf to the stem] indicates that the plant was picked in spring."

194

78. A theory was proposed in 1994 that Leonardo da Vinci faked the picture 350 years before the first known photograph was taken, by using a pinhole camera similar to those used to view solar eclipses. So far the theory remains merely speculation. The credibility of the book is also somewhat undermined by reliance upon an unnamed source who was stated to be a member of a secret sect that believes that Jesus did not die on the cross. The book is entitled *Turin Shroud: In Whose Image?* and was written by Lynn Picknett and Clive Prince.

79. Andrew Gumbel, "Ten Years on the Debunked Turin Shroud Gets a Second Coming," *Independent on Sunday,* Feb. 1, 1998; also see announcement by professor Alan Alder, a scientist attending a news conference in June 1997 to announce new conservation measures for the Shroud: "Expert Says Turin Shroud Older Than Tests Say," *Reuters,* 10 June 1997 (Turin, Italy), and results of his work described in *Unlocking the Secrets of the Shroud.* See also *The Blood and the Shroud,* p. 89.

80. *Unlocking the Secrets of the Shroud,* p. 99.

81. *The Blood and the Shroud,* pp. 90–92. The author, Ian Wilson, also independently confirmed the credibility of these conclusions with internationally known Thomas Loy, at Queensland University, Centre for Molecular and Cellular Biology. One of the researchers, Nancy Tryon, reported to Wilson that an insufficient number of base pairs (which are the basic units of DNA) have been isolated to permit any idea of cloning from the DNA.

82. The micrographs were taken by Vern Miller, an official professional photographer for the American scientific team at the 1978 International Congress on the Shroud of Turin, Italy. The chemical analysis was performed by Alan Adler, a professor of chemistry at Western Connecticut State University. See *Unlocking the Secrets of the Shroud,* pp. 52–62. Tests performed by Walter McCrone, a microanalyst, in 1978, convinced him that the samples were iron oxide, mixed with the pigment vermilion, used by artists. This work has been rebutted by John Heller, a professor of internal medicine and medical physics at Yale University, and research chemist, Dr. Alan Adler, of Western Connecticut State University. After extensive testing, Adler interpreted the results as "unequivocal evidence that [the samples from the bloodstains] were hemoglobin." See *The Blood and the Shroud,* pp. 83–93.

83. *Unlocking the Secrets of the Shroud*, pp. 57–58. For a unique discussion of the scientific evidence that has been produced with respect to the Shroud of Turin, see *Unlocking the Secrets of the Shroud*.

84. *Unlocking the Secrets of the Shroud*, pp. 89–111.

85. See *Unlocking the Secrets of the Shroud*; also see *The Bible as History*, pp. 355–356.

86. *The Digest of Justinian*, ed. Theodore Mommsen, Paul Krueger, Alan Watson (University of Pennsylvania Press, 1985), vol. 4, bk. 48, p. 863.

87. *Jesus: The Evidence*, p. 137.

88. *The Archeology of the New Testament*, pp. 261–263.

89. Ibid., pp. 261–266.

90. *Jesus: The Evidence*, p. 142.

91. Cyril of Jerusalem, "The Catechetical Lectures" (given in A.D. 348); Socrates, "Church History 1"; and Sozomen, "Church History 2"; all referenced in *The Archeology of the New Testament*, pp. 266–267.

92. *Jesus: The Evidence*, p. 142.

93. *Searching for Jesus*, p. 38; *The Archeology of the New Testament*, p. 267.

94. *Jesus: The Evidence*, p.142.

95. See *The Archeology of the New Testament*, p. 267; the testimony of the apostle John regarding the location of Gethsemane in a garden is found in John 19:41.

96. J. A. T. Robinson in *Redating The New Testament* dates this event at A.D. 33, and Raymond Brown in *Introduction to the New Testament* places it either between A.D. 30 and 34, or A.D. 36, according to various authorities. See *Redating the New Testament*, p. 44; *Introduction to the New Testament*, p. 428.

97. *Redating the New Testament*, p. 35.

98. F. F. Bruce, *The New Testament Documents: Are They Reliable?* p. 76.

99. Ibid., pp. 77–78.

100. *Introduction to the New Testament*, p. 512.

101. See Werner Keller, *The Bible as History* (William Morrow & Company, 1981), pp. 357–363.

102. *The New Testament Documents: Are They Reliable?*, p. 95.

Chapter 7

1. Letter from the emperor Trajan to Pliny (the Younger). "Plin. Epp. X. Xcvii," in *Documents of the Christian Church*, p. 4.
2. *Did Jesus Rise from the Dead? The Resurrection Debate*, p. 86.
3. *McCormick on Evidence*, vol. 2, Section 338, p. 433.
4. Quoted in Robert Shapiro, *Origins: A Skeptic's Guide to the Creation of Life on Earth* (Summit Books, a Division of Simon & Schuster, Inc. 1986), p. 127.
5. See *Darwin's Black Box*.
6. *Darwin's Black Box*, pp. 71–96.
7. Ibid., p. 194.
8. David J. Chalmers, *The Conscious Mind* (Oxford University Press, 1996), xiii–xiv. Chalmers claims to have no strong spiritual or religious inclinations. He holds that he is strongly inclined toward materialist explanations, but he has given up hope of finding one.
9. Michael B. Sabom, *Recollections of Death* (Harper & Row, 1982); Peter Fenwick and Elizabeth Fenwick, *The Truth in the Light* (Berkley Books, 1995); Kenneth Ring, *Heading Toward Omega* (Quill-William Morrow, 1984); Patrick Glynn, *God: the Evidence* (Prima Publishing, 1997).
10. *McCormick on Evidence*, vol. 2, Section 338, pp. 436–437.
11. *McCormick on Evidence*, vol. 2, Section 336.
12. *Pattern Jury Instructions (Civil Cases)*, Section 3.1, p. 30.
13. Peter delivered a speech in Jerusalem in which he said about Jesus: "This Man, delivered up by the predetermined plan and foreknowledge of God, you nailed to a cross by the hands of godless men and put Him to death. And God raised Him up again, putting an end to the agony of death, since it was impossible for Him to be held in its power."
14. An excellent analysis of the implications of the empty tomb was written in 1930, and has been reprinted ever since. See Frank Morison, *Who Moved the Stone?* (Zondervan Publishing House, 1958; reprint of the 1930 edition).
15. Lawrence Keppie, *The Making of the Roman Army* (B. T. Batsford Ltd., 1984), 38, 57.
16. Josh McDowell, *Evidence That Demands a Verdict* (Thomas Nelson Publishers, 1979), p. 209.
17. Eric Birley, *The Roman Army* (J. C. Gieben Publisher, 1988), 155.

18. "Military Law," in *The Digest of Justinian,* vol. 4, pp. 893, 895.
19. Alfred Edersheim, *The Temple: Its Ministry and Services* (Hendrickson Publishers, 1994), 112.
20. *Journal of the American Medical Association* (March 1, 1986), vol. 255, no. 11, pp. 1463. (Also see the footnotes listed in this article for further sources.)
21. Solomon Ganzfried, "Code of Jewish Law (Kitzur Schulchan Aruch)," translated by Hyman E. Goldin (New York: Hebrew Publishing Company, 1963), in *Unlocking the Secrets of the Shroud,* p. 73.
22. Ibid., pp. 65–75.
23. The quotation is from Werner Keller, *The Bible as History* (William Morrow and Company, Inc., 1981), 347; see Josephus, "Wars of the Jews," book 5, chap. 11,(1), in *The Complete Works of Josephus,* p. 565.
24. The statement is taken from Michael Behe's excellent book *Darwin's Black Box,* in which Behe, after a comprehensive examination of scientific literature, determined that not a single piece of scientific authority had been published to establish that complex biochemical systems at the molecular level could have evolved under random conditions of natural selection. The implication of the conclusion was that such irreducibly complex systems require intelligent design.

Chapter 8

1. I am indebted to Roger Penrose, professor of mathematics at the University of Oxford, for recognition of the beautiful analogy of the sympathetic vibration of instruments to the essence of the relationship between a parent and child, as set forth in his excellent book, *Shadows of the Mind.*

Suggested Reading

On the reliability of documentary evidence of the four Gospels, including the early dating of extant manuscripts, and analysis of the synoptic Gospels:

John A. T. Robinson, *Redating the New Testament* (Philadelphia: Westminster Press, 1976). Excellent discussion of the basis for a conclusion that each of the four Gospels was written well before the destruction of Jerusalem in A.D. 70. That conclusion is based upon a very well-reasoned analysis. This book contains detailed documentation of the source for each step in the reasoning process; it is particularly thorough. Apparently this work was an enormous surprise to biblical scholars because the author was well known for having a liberal view of the Gospels that would be expected to presuppose a later date for their authorship, as reflected in a popular work entitled *Honest to God.* That background, taken with the thorough analysis presented in this book, combines to lend great credibility to the conclusions presented. Information regarding books of the New Testament other than the four Gospels is also provided.

Philip Wesley Comfort, *The Origin of the Bible* (Tyndale House Publishers, 1992). Analysis of the development, compilation, and sources for the books of the Old and New Testaments of the Bible. Written clearly, this is an easy book to read and it is very informative. Comfort also includes a discussion of how the books of the Bible were chosen for inclusion, and thus determined to be canonical Scripture.

Carsten Peter Thiede and Matthew D'Ancona, *Eyewitness to Jesus* (Doubleday, 1996). Exciting description of the new early dating of the Magdalen fragments from the Gospel of Matthew, discussed at length in chapter 3, and the associated early dating of fragments from the Gospels of Luke and Mark. This book is written in a scholarly manner, detailed and well worth the extra effort required to read it from cover to cover. It is convincing primarily because of the detail provided regarding the process followed in the science of papyrology for determining the dates of manuscripts and fragments. As a bonus, the writer includes thoughtful analysis of the implications attached to the new early dating of the Gospels.

F. F. Bruce, *The New Testament Documents: Are They Reliable?* 5th rev. ed. (Intervarsity Press, 1997). F. F. Bruce was a highly regarded biblical scholar, and this book reflects the high quality of his work. It is a small paperback which is easy to read, and is crammed with information not easily obtained by the non-scholar.

Burton H. Throckmorton, Jr., ed., *Gospel Parallels: A Synopsis of the First Three Gospels*, 5th ed. (Nashville: Thomas Nelson 1992). While almost all books covering the subject of the origins of the Gospels and their reliability discuss the synoptic issue in a general fashion, this book actually compares word for word each passage of the Gospels of Matthew, Mark, and Luke side by side. Because the common passages in the three Gospels are not presented in the same order chronologically in the narratives, the work represents tremendous time and effort by the author. This book is an extremely valuable tool for those who do not want to rely upon interpretations by others. It presents the reader with the opportunity to analyze individually the so-called "synoptic problem" and reach independent conclusions regarding this issue. The study presented in chapter 4 is based upon the fourth edition of this work, with a preferred translation although this is not the latest edition. A valuable tool in analyzing what you find in this book in accordance with the analysis in chapter 4 is a side-by-side comparison of various translations of the Gospels such as *The Precise Parallel New Testament,* published by Oxford University Press.

On the "unknowables" of science:

Paul Davies, *The Mind of God: The Scientific Basis for a Rational World* (New York: Simon & Schuster, 1992). The author is a professor of mathematical physics, University of Adelaide, Australia. The scientific basis for the theory of the big bang event, the first cause, and order in the universe, as evidenced by the laws of physics and mathematics, are succinctly explained for the layman. The big bang event was the first event in the universe, and all space, time, and matter were created by that event. The big bang therefore creates a border to space and time. Sequential events are dependent upon each other— that is, they are based upon and ordered by cause and effect. Space and time are linked, and as events move forward, they create a chain of causal links, an arrow in time. Since cause precedes effect, and the effect itself resulted in space and time, then the first cause had to have occurred outside of the limitations of space and time. This is a scholarly exposition of the scientific basis for the premise that the world is intelligently designed. Although Davies does not go so far as to conclude that God has designed the universe, he does find that the laws of physics and mathematics seem to require a belief that the universe evidences processing according to "some ingenious pre-existing set of rules." The book is written for readers without scientific training; however, it is very detailed and requires concentration.

Hugh Ross, *The Creator and the Cosmos* (Colorado Springs: NavPress, 1993). Hugh Ross is an astrophysicist. He has compiled recent scientific evidence of an ordered and intelligently designed universe. Dramatic cosmological breakthroughs that shed new light on our view of the universe, beginning with discoveries from findings of the Cosmic Background Explorer (COBE) satellite in 1992, are presented to the reader. Again, while the book is written for lay readers, it does require focus as it is extremely, but necessarily, detailed.

201

Discussions of the big bang theory and the space-time theorem, together with evident design of the universe, led Ross to conclude that this "proof of the beginning of time may rank as the most theologically significant theorem of all time."

Michael J. Behe, *Darwin's Black Box: The Biochemical Challenge to Evolution* (The Free Press, 1996). This is an excellent book, well worth the read. Michael Behe has thoroughly proven under rigorous standards that the human biochemical system cannot have been formed by numerous, successive, slight modifications. The proof of that conclusion is very complex and is discussed in detail, but in terms understandable to a lay reader, using analogies such as the interdependence of the parts on a simple mousetrap, and the Rube Goldberg contraption described in chapter 7, as well as actual descriptions of such biochemical systems at the cellular level as the human immune system, and the blood-clotting system. This book does not question Darwin's theory of evolution on a macro level, but it has shifted the burden of proof regarding random evolution of microsystems to proponents of that hypothesis, and will require the presentation of equivalent empirical evidence to controvert Behe's conclusions.

Robert Shapiro, *Origins: A Skeptic's Guide to the Creation of Life* (Summit Books, 1986). A thorough description of various contemporary theories for how life began, with a discussion of the strengths and weaknesses of each one. This is a well-written book that is understandable to the layperson. The author, a leading authority on origin of life research, has demonstrated that all of the theories are based upon unproven assumptions. Shapiro has no religious agenda, and the focus is on the scientific method; however, his conclusion is that the current status of origin of life theories and research falls into a category that he has called "bio-mythology."

Charles B. Thaxton, Walter L. Bradley, and Roger L. Olsen, *The Mystery of Life's Origin* (Lewis and Stanley, 1984; second printing, 1992). This is a clearly written summary of the status of experimental work on chemical evolution of the origin of life, with a well-reasoned conclusion that chemical evolution is highly implausible. The authors have noted the fact that experimental conditions in many of these studies have been so simplified, and so many assumptions have been made, that the studies have no real relevance to the actual conditions which existed on primitive earth. Dean H. Kenyon, professor of biology at San Francisco State University, has stated in the "Foreword" what the studies thereafter have shown: "No experimental system yet devised has provided the slightest clue as to how biologically meaningful sequences of subunits might have originated in prebiotic polynucleotides or polypeptides."

Cosmos, Bios, Theos: Scientists Reflect on Science, God, and the Origins of the Universe, Life and Homo Sapiens), edited by Henry Margenau and Roy Abraham Varghese (Open Court Publishing Company, a division of Carus Publishing, 1992; fourth printing, 1997). This interesting book presents the conclusions of seventy distinguished scientists, including twenty Nobel Prize winners, on the relationship between science and religion. The perspective of each, in some degree, is that scientific truth can be reconciled with a religious interpretation of the world. A mixture of personal reflections, essays, and interview-type questions and answers, the book is divided into four parts. The subject matter of the four divisions provides a full picture of the offering. part 1 is a composition of thoughts of astronomers, mathematicians and physicists on specific issues; part 2 is a similar presentation by biologists and chemists; part 3 contains a debate by eight philosophers, historians, and theologians on the existence of God and the origin of the universe. Part 4 provides concluding scientific postscripts on the origin of the universe, and relativity, quantum theory, and the mystery of life. This is easy to read and very informative.

On the mystery of human consciousness and the question of a soul:

Roger Penrose, *Shadows of the Mind: A Search for the Missing Science of Consciousness* (Oxford University Press, 1994). Roger Penrose is the Rouse Ball professor of mathematics at the University of Oxford. This book establishes a clear and detailed rebuttal to the theory that human consciousness can be reduced to physical computation, similar to the programming of a computer. Penrose has recognized that an essential ingredient is missing from our current understanding of consciousness; however, he maintains that this missing essence will someday be understood by science. As of today, however, Penrose has concluded that there is not a physical, biological, or computational theory capable of explaining human intelligence and consciousness. In other words, as stated in chapter 7, we are more than the sum of our physical parts. While the book is beautifully written, it is somewhat difficult to follow in parts without a mathematical background. Penrose has attempted to relegate the more difficult proofs to an ancillary position in the development of his theory, and in this he has been somewhat successful. A reader with little mathematical background can still enjoy and understand the book.

[For an understanding of the opposing position that what we know as consciousness is nothing more than the computational ability of the physical brain, see Daniel C. Dennett, *Consciousness Explained* (Boston: Little, Brown and Company, 1991).]

David C. Chalmers, *The Conscious Mind* (Oxford University Press, 1996). The author is a professor of philosophy at the University of California, Santa Cruz. His work is framed by the assumption that consciousness is a natural phenomenon that is governed by natural laws, but he states that while there must be some correct scientific theory of consciousness, it has not yet been developed. Chalmers is strongly inclined toward materialist reductive explanations for consciousness, and he states in the introduction that in preparing this book he had hoped for a materialist theory. On the other hand, he has concluded that "if a physicist or a cognitive scientist suggests that consciousness can be explained in physical terms, this is merely a hope ungrounded in current theory, and the question remains open." Portions of this book are difficult to read, but the author provides a guide to the reader who wishes to avoid technicalities.

The Cambridge Companion to Descartes, edited by John Cottingham (Cambridge University Press, 1992; last reprinted in 1995). This will provide an excellent source for those interested in the intellectual background for the dualistic theory of mind—that is, a view that the mind operates independent of the physical body. Descartes's thinking provided the catalyst for almost all current debate on the subject of the mystery of consciousness, even for those who argue that his theories are discredited.

Suggested Reading

Douglas R. Hofstadter, *Godel, Escher, Bach: An Eternal Golden Braid* (New York: Vintage Books, 1989). This fascinating book is described by the author as "A Metaphorical Fugue on Minds and Machines in the Spirit of Lewis Carroll." It is a beautifully written study through the use of musical, mathematical, and pictorial models of the essential ingredient of consciousness that is unexplained today. The common element in music, math, and the pictures of the graphic artist, Escher, is the phenomenon which occurs in each of these areas when "by moving upwards (or downwards) through the levels of some hierarchical system, we unexpectedly find ourselves right back where we started." These are "Strange Loops." In music the subject system is musical keys and is exemplified by the beauty and complexity of the music of Bach; in mathematics it is present in mathematical reasoning and logic, as expressed by Godel's Theorem; and in the work of Escher it is present in his drawings, which provide double meanings through illusions. Many of these drawings are provided for the reader. This book is an intellectually stimulating work of art.

Michael B. Sabom, *Recollections of Death: A Medical Investigation* (New York: Harper & Row, 1982). Michael Sabom is a cardiologist who conducted an extensive medical investigation into claims of patients who claimed to have had a "near-death experience." He began the investigation as a skeptic bothered by the unsystematic and anecdotal method of reporting these claims in early books on the subject. In this study he particularly focused upon verification through medical records and other corroborating evidence regarding details revealed by subjects that would not be understood or known to people without medical training. Some of the specific case studies set forth by Sabom are extremely convincing by their detail and his method of substantiation, particularly as to the portion of the experience referred to as "autoscopic"—that is, claims by survivors that they actually perceived things in the operating room from a physical position different than that of the unconscious body prior to resuscitation. In certain cases he found that there was no plausible explanation for the accuracy of the observations, as corroborated, other than the occurrence of a split between the mind and the physical brain. He was left with the question whether this mind which appears to have split apart from the physical brain could be a soul.

Peter Fenwick and Elizabeth A. Fenwick, *The Truth in the Light* (A Berkeley Book, 1995). Peter Fenwick is a British neuropsychiatrist; Elizabeth Fenwick, his wife, is an author who has written several books for the British Medical Association. Although the authors rely heavily on anecdotal evidence, the book is well written and provides excellent reports on the current state of research into near-death experiences. The approach here is to seek an explanation for the experience in terms of biology and psychiatry, particularly on the question of the mind/brain split implied by the research of Michael Sabom. From a scientific viewpoint the "mind" should not be able to process information or to transfer it to memory if it were separated from the physical brain. Current scientific explanations that these are tricks of the brain don't satisfy because you would expect major discrepancies to exist between the psychological image and the real image. Fenwick explores these issues and others in great detail, and provides convincing refutation of current theories of physical causes, such as lack of oxygen and random activity in the brain. This book provides an excellent analysis and study of the near-death experience and its implications for the mysterious essence of consciousness.

On archaeological evidence and artifacts:

Jack Finegan, *The Archeology of the New Testament* (Princeton University Press, 1992). This excellent and scholarly work provides the most extensive compilation found of information on archaeological discoveries in the times and at the place that the Gospels were written. It is easy to read but provides great detail, including photographs of archaeological sites, together with drawings and maps. Related historical sources help the reader to identify and interpret the objects and sites uncovered. This book is a treasure.

Ian Wilson, *Jesus: The Evidence* (HarperSanFrancisco, 1996). The author is a journalist who lives in Australia. This book provides an easy-to-read source of information on manuscripts of the New Testament and selected archaeological discoveries. The general discussion on the manuscripts and historical corroboration of early Christianity is somewhat colored by the author's view and does not reach the scholarly depth of reasoning and analysis provided in the books recommended above on the reliability of the manuscripts. The archaeological information is somewhat selective and suffers in contrast to other sources available to the reader that provide more interesting detail; however, that does not diminish the beauty of the presentation, which includes many stunning color photographs. The author also just published an excellent new book on the Shroud of Turin that is discussed below.

Walter E. Rast, *Through the Ages in Palestinian Archaeology* (Trinity Press International, 1992). This is a very good handbook for the general reader. It covers the earliest period of the stone age in Palestine, through the early centuries of this era, with brief views through the present time. The reader is provided with guidance on what the practice of archaeology includes, how archaeological expeditions work, what archaeologists are looking for, and how things are dated, as well as actual descriptions of the excavations and discoveries. This is easy reading and very informative.

Ian Wilson, *The Blood and the Shroud* (The Free Press, a division of Simon & Schuster Inc., 1998). This excellent book contains discussions of the latest evidence that the Shroud of Turin is actually the linen cloth which wrapped the body of Jesus of Nazareth in the first century. Wonderful photographs are included. The presentation is very objective, and opposing viewpoints and evidence are presented for consideration. Although the question of the validity of the shroud remains unresolved, the positive evidence presented by Wilson for its authenticity is very convincing.

Gilbert R. Lavoie, *Unlocking the Secrets of the Shroud* (ThomasMore, 1998). The author is a specialist in internal and occupational medicine. The medical and scientific evidence is presented carefully and in detail; however, the conclusions incorporate an important scriptural perspective as well. For example, an apparent inconsistency between the presence of blood on the shroud and the Jewish practice of washing the body of all blood prior to burial was reconciled through the author's discovery that an exception under Jewish law existed for the person who died a violent death. In that case, the victim's body was simply placed in a cloth and buried, without cleansing. This book provides a very interesting and different approach to a study of evidence for the authenticity of the shroud.

Biblical Archaeology Review is a popular magazine available on newsstands and in many libraries. *Near Eastern Archaeology* and *BASOR* are two journals generally available in large libraries that are also highly recommended sources for very interesting and reliable information on archaeological corroboration for the testimony of the Gospels.

On the paradox of Mozart, providing hints of the unknown:

Letters of Wolfgang Amadeus Mozart. Selected and edited by Hans Mersmann; translated from the German by M. M. Bozman (Dover Publications, Inc., New York). This book contains a reprint of the most interesting of Mozart's correspondence to relatives and friends. Mozart was a prolific letter writer and many of his letters have been preserved. His letters are very personal, described by the editor of this book as "unstudied, non-literary, conversational" with wildly erratic spelling, punctuation, and grammar. They are most interesting because they reveal the true personality of the great composer, and they truly evidence the great paradox between the music created by this genius, and the disorder of his life.

Alfred Einstein, *Mozart: His Character, His Work*, translated by Arthur Mendel and Nathan Broder (Oxford University Press, 1945). This is one of the definitive biographies of Mozart, written by a great scholar. It is a comprehensive story of the life of Mozart and his interaction with people who were important in his life. An introductory quote of the author is informative: "There is a strange kind of human being in whom there is an eternal struggle between body and soul, animal and god, for dominance. In all great men this mixture is striking, and in none more than Wolfgang Amadeus Mozart."

Wolfgang Hildesheimer, *Mozart,* translated from German by Marion Faber (Farrar Straus Giroux, 1982). This biography offers a revealing portrait of Mozart, organized in thematic sections in a manner which focuses on issues in the composer's life. Interesting portraits are included as well as details which are not found in many of the more orthodox biographies. For example, the name by which the author reports that the composer is well known today—Amadeus—originated from a joke signature he used on some of his letters: *Wolfgangus Amadeus Mozartus.*

Arthur Hutchings, *Mozart: The Man, the Musician* (Schirmer Books, A Division of Macmillan Publishing Co., Inc., 1976.) A beautiful book, full of color pictures and portraits of Mozart, his family, and the cities in which he lived. The first part of this book is a biography, which includes an interesting analysis of the musician. The second portion of the book focuses on the music itself and the creative process. This is an excellent, overall view of Mozart and his work.

In addition to the foregoing, the following books are highly recommended for general reading:

Frank Morrison, *Who Moved the Stone?* (Zondervan Publishing House, 1958). This book, first published in 1930 by a different publisher, contains an extremely well-reasoned analysis of the validity of the testimony of the Gospels that the resurrection did occur. The investigation covers the trial of Jesus, the crucifixion, burial, and resurrection and is primarily based upon logical analysis of the narratives of the Gospels—that is, what occurred and when, and what is reasonable to presume and what is irrational to suppose. The discussion relies upon evidence provided by harmonizing various portions of the Scriptures measured against historical and religious facts. The author was a British journalist, and the method of investigation evidences that perspective.

Patrick Glynn, *God: The Evidence* (Forum. An imprint of Prima Publishing, 1997). This is a philosophical presentation of scientific support for the existence of an intelligent creator of the universe. In addition to an overview of current scientific evidence for the existence of something transcending the physical world, the author provides an analysis of the relationship as it stands today between psychology and religious thought, and that of medicine and faith. The author is the associate director and scholar in residence at the George Washington University Institute for Communitarian Policy Studies in Washington, D.C.

Jesus Under Fire, edited by Michael J. Wilkins and J. P. Moreland (Zondervan Publishing House, 1995). This book is primarily a response to the current popular thought that attempts to place the Gospel testimony regarding Jesus of Nazareth within the "myths and legends" theory discussed in our case. It is particularly directed as a rebuttal to the fellows of a group which has called itself "The Jesus Seminar," formed in 1985 to reach a "scholarly consensus" on the historical authenticity of the statements attributed to Jesus in the Gospels. The findings of The Jesus Seminar are dissected with precision and refuted through eight well-researched essays by scholars expert in philosophy, biblical studies, and apologetics. The insufficiency of the process by which the findings of The Jesus Seminar were achieved is illuminated through the analysis presented in our case.

C. S. Lewis, *The Case for Christianity* (Macmillan Publishing Company, 1989). C. S. Lewis was a scholar and theologian who taught English literature at Magdalen College, Oxford. He was a prolific writer, and some may be surprised to learn that he was the author of several classic children's books, including *The Silver Chair* and the *Chronicles of Narnia*. *The Case for Christianity* provides a basic discussion of Christian belief in a concise and witty manner. Beginning with a discussion of the absolute standards of right and wrong, which may be thought of as the law of human nature, Lewis progresses to an unusual discussion of what Christians believe, without involving questions relating to particular dogma. If you enjoy this book, you will also enjoy two other works by C. S. Lewis, *Mere Christianity* and *Surprised by Joy*.